Understanding World History

The Making of the Atomic Bomb

Other titles in the series include:

Ancient Chinese Dynasties
Ancient Egypt
Ancient Greece
Ancient Rome
The Black Death
The Decade of the 2000s
The Digital Age
The Early Middle Ages
Elizabethan England
The Enlightenment
The Great Recession
The History of Rock and Roll
The History of Slavery
The Holocaust
The Industrial Revolution
The Late Middle Ages
Pearl Harbor
The Renaissance
The Rise of Islam
The Rise of the Nazis
Victorian England

Understanding World History

The Making of the Atomic Bomb

Hal Marcovitz

Bruno Leone
Series Consultant

ReferencePoint Press®

San Diego, CA

ReferencePoint Press®

Printed in the United States

For more information, contact:
ReferencePoint Press, Inc.
PO Box 27779
San Diego, CA 92198
www. ReferencePointPress.com

LIBRARY OF CONGRESS CATALOGING-IN-PUBLICATION DATA

Marcovitz, Hal.
The making of the atomic bomb / by Hal Marcovitz.
pages cm. -- (Understanding world history)
Includes bibliographical references and index.
ISBN-13: 978-1-60152-686-1 (hardback)
ISBN-10: 1-60152-686-5 (hardback)
1. Atomic bomb--United States--History--Juvenile literature. 2. Manhattan Project (U.S.)--History--Juvenile literature. I. Title.
QC773.3.U5M28 2015
623.4'5119--dc23

2014001543

Contents

Foreword

When the Puritans first emigrated from England to America in 1630, they believed that their journey was blessed by a covenant between themselves and God. By the terms of that covenant they agreed to establish a community in the New World dedicated to what they believed was the true Christian faith. God, in turn, would reward their fidelity by making certain that they and their descendants would always experience his protection and enjoy material prosperity. Moreover, the Lord guaranteed that their land would be seen as a shining beacon—or in their words, a "city upon a hill,"—which the rest of the world would view with admiration and respect. By embracing this notion that God could and would shower his favor and special blessings upon them, the Puritans were adopting the providential philosophy of history—meaning that history is the unfolding of a plan established or guided by a higher intelligence.

The concept of intercession by a divine power is only one of many explanations of the driving forces of world history. Historians and philosophers alike have subscribed to numerous other ideas. For example, the ancient Greeks and Romans argued that history is cyclical. Nations and civilizations, according to these ancients of the Western world, rise and fall in unpredictable cycles; the only certainty is that these cycles will persist throughout an endless future. The German historian Oswald Spengler (1880–1936) echoed the ancients to some degree in his controversial study *The Decline of the West.* Spengler asserted that all civilizations inevitably pass through stages comparable to the life span of a person: childhood, youth, adulthood, old age, and, eventually, death. As the title of his work implies, Western civilization is currently entering its final stage.

Joining those who see purpose and direction in history are thinkers who completely reject the idea of meaning or certainty. Rather, they reason that since there are far too many random and unseen factors at work on the earth, historians would be unwise to endorse historical predictability of any type. Warfare (both nuclear and conventional), plagues, earthquakes, tsunamis, meteor showers, and other catastrophic world-changing events have loomed large throughout history and prehistory. In his essay "A Free Man's Worship," philosopher and mathematician

Bertrand Russell (1872–1970) supported this argument, which many refer to as the nihilist or chaos theory of history. According to Russell, history follows no preordained path. Rather, the earth itself and all life on earth resulted from, as Russell describes it, an "accidental collocation of atoms." Based on this premise, he pessimistically concluded that all human achievement will eventually be "buried beneath the debris of a universe in ruins."

Whether history does or does not have an underlying purpose, historians, journalists, and countless others have nonetheless left behind a record of human activity tracing back nearly 6,000 years. From the dawn of the great ancient Near Eastern civilizations of Mesopotamia and Egypt to the modern economic and military behemoths China and the United States, humanity's deeds and misdeeds have been and continue to be monitored and recorded. The distinguished British scholar Arnold Toynbee (1889–1975), in his widely acclaimed twelve-volume work entitled *A Study of History,* studied twenty-one different civilizations that have passed through history's pages. He noted with certainty that others would follow.

In the final analysis, the academic and journalistic worlds mostly regard history as a record and explanation of past events. From a more practical perspective, history represents a sequence of building blocks—cultural, technological, military, and political—ready to be utilized and enhanced or maligned and perverted by the present. What that means is that all societies—whether advanced civilizations or preliterate tribal cultures—leave a legacy for succeeding generations to either embrace or disregard.

Recognizing the richness and fullness of history, the ReferencePoint Press Understanding World History series fosters an evaluation and interpretation of history and its influence on later generations. Each volume in the series approaches its subject chronologically and topically, with specific focus on nations, periods, or pivotal events. Primary and secondary source quotations are included, along with complete source notes and suggestions for further research.

Moreover, the series reflects the truism that the key to understanding the present frequently lies in the past. With that in mind, each series title concludes with a legacy chapter that highlights the bonds between past and present and, more important, demonstrates that world history is a continuum of peoples and ideas, sometimes hidden but there nonetheless, waiting to be discovered by those who choose to look.

Important Events in the Making of the Atomic Bomb

1900 ••• 1930 1935 1940

1905
Albert Einstein publishes the equation $E=mc^2$, essentially the mathematical explanation for how matter can be converted into energy.

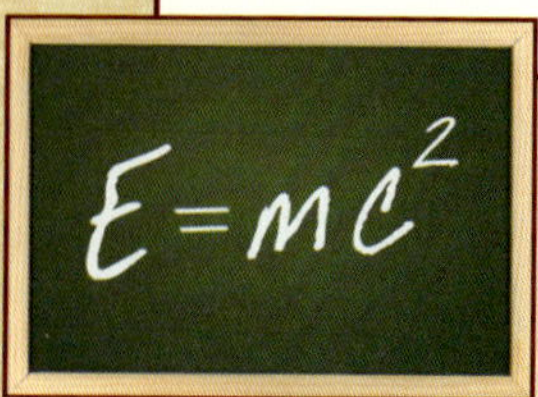

1933
Physicist Leo Szilard conceives the process of fission, suggesting that a chain reaction can be created by separating neutrons from atomic nuclei.

1938
German chemists Otto Hahn and Fritz Strassmann bombard uranium atoms with neutrons, confirming that chain reactions can cause the release of energy.

1939
Einstein writes a letter to US president Franklin D. Roosevelt, calling the president's attention to the German fission program and urging the creation of a US government–sponsored program to pursue fission and develop an atomic bomb; Roosevelt responds by establishing the Advisory Committee on Uranium.

1941
On December 7, Japanese planes attack the US Navy base at Pearl Harbor, Hawaii, drawing America into World War II.

1942
In September US Army general Leslie Groves is named to head what is now known as the Manhattan Project; Groves asks physicist J. Robert Oppenheimer to serve as civilian director of the atomic bomb program.
On December 2, a Manhattan Project experiment under the direction of physicist Enrico Fermi successfully controls fission.

1943
The Manhattan Project establishes a central laboratory near Los Alamos, New Mexico; on February 27, a group of Norwegian commandos sabotage the German heavy water plant at Vemork, Norway, severely damaging the Nazi program to develop atomic weapons.

1944
In September the US Army 509th Composite Group begins training for the mission of dropping atomic bombs on enemy cities.

1945
On June 1, President Harry Truman decides to use atomic bombs on Japanese cities to end the war in the Pacific. On July 16, Manhattan Project scientists stage the Trinity test near Alamogordo, New Mexico, detonating the first atomic bomb, a plutonium-fueled weapon. On August 6, the B-29 bomber *Enola Gay* drops an atomic bomb on the city of Hiroshima, Japan, leveling the city and immediately killing sixty-eight thousand people. After a second bomb is dropped on August 9, the Japanese surrender.

2013
Iran agrees to halt its uranium-enrichment program following years of harsh economic sanctions leveled by Western countries.

1950 1975 2000

1962
For thirteen days in October, the United States and the Soviet Union teeter on the brink of atomic warfare after the Americans learn the Soviets have established nuclear missile bases in Cuba; the Soviets ultimately agree to dismantle the bases.

2003
The United States initiates an invasion of Iraq under the belief that dictator Saddam Hussein is pursuing a nuclear weapons program.

1953
Julius and Ethel Rosenberg, found guilty of leaking atomic secrets to the Soviets, are executed.

1949
On August 29, the Soviet Union conducts a test of an atomic bomb, touching off the Cold War.

Introduction

The Defining Characteristics of the Making of the Atomic Bomb

The British author and historian H.G. Wells is best known for his science-fiction novel *The War of the Worlds*, in which human civilization must respond to hostile Martian invaders, but in 1914 Wells published another, lesser-known novel in which he prophesized terrible events. In his book *The World Set Free*, Wells foretold eruption of worldwide warfare. Moreover, aerial combat was employed in the war, and so was the use of atomic bombs. "All through the nineteenth and twentieth centuries the amount of energy that men were able to command was continually increasing," Wells wrote. "Applied to warfare that meant that the power to inflict a blow, the power to destroy, was continually increasing. There was no increase whatever in the ability to escape. Every sort of passive defence, armour, fortifications, and so forth, was being outmastered by this tremendous increase on the destructive side."[1]

In Wells's story, armies destroy entire cities by dropping atomic bombs from aircraft. At the time Wells published the novel, aviation was in its infancy—the Wright brothers had made the first engine-powered flight just eleven years earlier. Airplanes were, at this stage, mostly tiny experimental craft, capable of short-duration flights only, and hardly able to transport huge and heavy bombs. And yet Wells had correctly deduced that some three decades later an army would use airplanes to drop atomic bombs on target cities.

Atomic science was in its infancy as well. In his book, Wells predicted that the splitting of the atom, a chemical reaction known as fission, would produce an enormous amount of explosive energy—enough energy to level a city. But when Wells had published the book, the splitting of the atom had occurred in theory only. The first actual fission reaction would be created in a laboratory twenty-four years *after* the publication of Wells's book. The first experiment in which scientists controlled the fission reaction—a vital step in the creation of the atomic bomb—would not occur until four years after that.

The Pursuit of Fission

The World Set Free received positive reviews—a book critic for the *New York Times* called it "a magnificent piece of workmanship"[2]—but the book suffered mediocre sales. And yet, although many members of the public declined to read the book, it would for many years find wide readership among the scientific community. In 1932 the Hungarian-born physicist Leo Szilard discovered the book, and after reading the story elected to devote his talents to the pursuit of fission.

Until then, Szilard had studied X-rays and had even developed a new method for commercial refrigeration. After reading Wells's story, however, he realized the horrific ramifications should the secret of creating fission fall into the wrong hands. By this time Szilard had immigrated to England. He had been living and working in Germany for many years, but the rise to power of the anti-Semitic Nazis forced Szilard and other Jewish scientists to flee. Wells's story convinced Szilard that the free nations of the world would be in a race against the Nazis and other totalitarian societies to develop the atomic bomb. Says Anne Rooney, a historian for the University of Essex in Great Britain, "Leó Szilárd was inspired by a novel written by the British writer H.G. Wells, called *The World Set Free*, in which a new type of weapon, an 'atomic bomb,' wrought devastation. . . . Szilárd envisioned the [bomb] as a way of protecting the world against the destruction described by Wells as he hoped the bomb would be used as a threat and not actually used."[3]

After moving to England Szilard was given lab space at St. Bartholomew's Hospital in London, where he researched the chemical reactions—known as radioactivity—of highly volatile elements. In 1933 the physicist conceived the process of the chain reaction in the atomic nuclei—the process in which neutrons break away from their atoms, forming new nuclei and then breaking away again. This process constitutes fission. Said Szilard, "If we could find an element which is split by neutrons . . . such an element, if assembled in sufficiently large mass, could sustain a nuclear chain reaction."[4]

The Manhattan Project

Szilard would eventually move to the United States, where he joined a community of scientists in researching atomic fission. By the end of the 1930s, as World War II erupted in Europe, these scientists helped convince President Franklin D. Roosevelt of the need for government support for the development of the atomic bomb. Roosevelt, suspecting that America would soon be drawn into the war, authorized an unprecedented government project in which the talents of hundreds of scientists were pooled with the singular goal of developing the most devastating weapon known to human civilization.

This effort, known as the Manhattan Project, would be unlike any scientific project undertaken in history. Until the Manhattan Project, science was pursued under public purview: Scientists gave lectures about their work, published their findings in academic journals available for public consumption, and often made headlines with their discoveries. In contrast, the Manhattan Project was pursued under the most secretive of conditions. Eventually those involved in the project would work together under tight security in a secret lab complex erected in a remote New Mexico desert.

Nevertheless, the scientists who joined this effort knew they were in a race against the Nazis and America's other enemy, the Japanese, to develop the bomb first. Certainly they knew the awesome destruction their work could release on human society, but like Szilard, they hoped

A mushroom cloud forms during atomic weapons testing. Working under tight security in a secret lab in a remote section of New Mexico desert, scientists affiliated with the Manhattan Project developed the atomic bomb.

the bomb would be used as a deterrent. They hoped that once America possessed the bomb, the Germans and Japanese would realize the futility of continuing the war and surrender.

And so they pursued the development of the atomic bomb, joining this secret mission and putting aside their personal doubts about whether their work ran counter to their moral responsibilities as scientists. According to Gerard J. DeGroot, a historian at the University of St. Andrews in Scotland,

> In the race to build the bomb, scientists trampled over their moral doubts and muddied the noble traditions of the profession. . . . The liberal ethic guiding scientists conflicted with the pragmatic authoritarianism by which states conduct war. It chafed them—especially those who had escaped repressive regimes—to work in secrecy, not to mention to watch the noble goal of discovery superseded by the coarse practical purpose of building a weapon.[5]

Chapter 1

What Conditions Led to the Making of the Atomic Bomb?

The study of the atom dates back at least to the fifth century BCE, when the Greek philosopher Democritus suggested—quite accurately—that all matter is made up of tiny particles and, in fact, these particles are so small that they cannot be seen. But there were some flaws in Democritus's theories. For starters, he named these particles *atoms*, after the Greek word *atomos*, which translates roughly into "that which cannot be split." It would take roughly twenty-five hundred years, but eventually scientists would prove Democritus wrong.

By the eighteenth and nineteenth centuries European society was enjoying the fruits of the Enlightenment—an era of tremendous advancement in literature, education, the arts, and science. Scientists of this era started forming new theories based on their observations of nature and experiments they were able to carry out using the rudimentary methods available to them. In 1703 Isaac Newton of England proposed that all mass is constantly in motion—a significant component of the theory that neutrons can be propelled away from their nuclei. In 1803 John Dalton of England found that different atoms have different weights. Moreover, Dalton also suggested that atoms can be combined, rearranged, and separated during chemical reactions—again, a significant step in the theory that chain reactions could be sparked in the nuclei of atoms. In 1898 the Polish-born French chemist Marie Curie found that some chemical elements are radioactive, meaning they emit particles. Curie performed experiments in measuring the energy dissipated by the element uranium, which would have an enormous impact on atomic science and the making of the bomb.

In 1905 the German-born mathematician Albert Einstein published the equation $E=mc^2$, meaning energy equals mass multiplied by the square of the speed of light. In its simplest terms, the equation means that under the right circumstances energy and mass are interchangeable: Energy can become mass, and mass can become energy. According to Einstein's calculations, even the tiniest particles—atoms—contain enormous amounts of energy. Einstein determined that when mass is converted into energy, it will move at the square of the speed of light. Therefore, when changing mass into energy, the square of the speed of light is the conversion factor when determining how much energy is contained in a particle of mass. Since the speed of light squared is a huge number—some 55.9 billion miles (90 billion km) per second—it was evident to Einstein, and to the scientists who would build upon his work and develop the atomic bomb, that they could produce an enormous amount of destructive energy from a very small piece of matter. "It is not improbable," Einstein said, "that from this will come new energy sources of enormous power."[6]

The Inefficient Proton

Following Einstein's work, other scientists would make their own contributions to fission research. In 1910 the New Zealand–born British scientist Ernest Rutherford found that atoms are composed of nuclei, and in 1920 he suggested that nuclei are composed of neutrons—particles that hold no electrical charge. Lacking an electrical charge, Rutherford suggested, neutrons could pass from nucleus to nucleus unrestrained by the electrical forces found in atoms.

As scientists such as Rutherford and Einstein proposed equations and theories, others were doing more practical work—creating devices that would help advance the science of fission research. In 1929

American physicist Ernest O. Lawrence developed the cyclotron, a device that enables researchers to accelerate the speed of atomic particles. Another important device developed during this era was the particle accelerator. Both devices enable scientists to study the motions of atomic particles—an important step in creating fission. Two British scientists, John Cockcroft and Ernest Walton, built the particle accelerator

Albert Einstein, pictured here in 1922, realized that atoms contain enormous amounts of energy. He and other scientists came to understand that a very tiny piece of matter could be used to produce destructive energy on a massive scale.

in 1932. It was essentially a gun that fired protons—the electrically charged components of the nuclei—at a mass of the element lithium. Each time a lithium atom was struck by a proton, it split the atom into two, forming an atom of helium. The particle accelerator had succeeded in splitting the atom and releasing energy, adding legitimacy to the theory that atoms were not indestructible. However, it was quickly determined that protons did a poor job of splitting the atom. Just 1 in 10 million protons were believed to survive the impact with the nuclei, meaning this method of splitting the atom was highly inefficient and uncontrollable. Employing protons to spark a chain reaction was soon discarded as a viable method of attaining fission. However, while Cockcroft and Walton experimented with protons, other scientists were studying the use of neutrons in attaining fission.

The Discovery of the Neutron

Since 1920, when Rutherford proposed the existence of the neutron, the particle existed in theory only. During this era atoms were known to contain two components—electrons, which carry a negative electrical charge, and protons, which carry a positive charge. In 1932 British scientist James Chadwick announced that his experiments had confirmed the existence of a third particle, the neutron, which contains no electrical charge. An assistant to Rutherford, Chadwick had been carrying out experiments of his own.

There had actually been experiments conducted prior to Chadwick's announcement in which a neutral force was found in the atom. Experiments conducted by Marie Curie's daughter, Irène Joliot-Curie, and her husband, Frédéric Joliot, suggested that this neutral force was composed of gamma rays—radiation given off by the atom. The Joliots produced evidence of the emission of gamma rays by exposing various metals and other materials to the radioactive element beryllium.

Chadwick was skeptical of these findings and decided to test them using methods he devised. Chadwick constructed a tube. At one end of the tube he placed a small mass of beryllium; the other end contained a variety of metals, among them lithium, boron, and carbon. He also pumped

Lise Meitner

Following World War II, Lise Meitner expressed guilt for her role in enabling Otto Hahn and Fritz Strassmann to achieve a fission reaction in their laboratory, but she also heaped harsh criticism on Hahn and Strassmann for pursuing their experiments under a Nazi regime. In June 1945—a month after the fall of the Nazis—Meitner wrote to Hahn, saying, "You all worked for Nazi Germany. And you tried to offer only a passive resistance. Certainly, to buy off your conscience you helped here and there a persecuted person, but millions of innocent human beings were allowed to be murdered without any protest being uttered."

Born in Austria in 1878, Meitner earned a doctoral degree in physics at the University of Vienna in 1905. During World War I, Meitner volunteered to aid the army of Austria-Hungary, working as an X-ray technician. After the war she headed the physics department at the Kaiser Wilhelm Institute for Chemistry in Germany. Born into a Jewish family, Meitner converted to a Protestant denomination, but this fact mattered little to the Nazis, who still considered her Jewish. Fearing for her life, Meitner fled to Sweden in 1938. She was later approached by American officials who offered her a position with the Manhattan Project. She turned them down, declaring, "I will have nothing to do with a bomb!" Meitner died in Great Britain in 1968.

Quoted in John Cornwell, *Hitler's Scientists: Science, War, and the Devil's Pact.* New York: Penguin Compass, 2003, e-book.

Quoted in Ruth Lewin Sime, *Lise Meitner: A Life in Physics.* Berkeley: University of California Press, 1996, p. 279.

several gases into the chamber—nitrogen, hydrogen, helium, oxygen, and argon were all tested. As radiation from beryllium struck the targeted metals and gases, Chadwick measured the collisions on an oscilloscope, a device featuring a screen that gauges electrical activity by displaying images in peaks and valleys. Whenever a new substance was introduced into the tube, the oscilloscope recorded new peaks and valleys. Essentially the oscilloscope was recording a transfer of energy from the beryllium to the lithium, boron, nitrogen, and other substances at the far end of the tube. Since gamma rays were believed to spark little significant electrical activity, there had to be another explanation for the spikes whenever the beryllium radiation struck the targeted metals or gases.

Chadwick deduced that this energy transfer, from the beryllium to the targeted metals and gases, was carried out by a particle that easily could move from substance to substance. Hence, this particle carried no electrical charge of its own that would impede its path, causing it to be absorbed by the nuclei of beryllium atoms at one end of the tube. Chadwick saw this experiment as confirmation of Rutherford's theory that atoms contained a third, neutrally charged component: the neutron. The Italian physicist Emilio Segrè commented, "When [the neutron] was ultimately there he perceived it immediately, clearly and convincingly. These are the marks of a great experimental physicist."[7]

The Liquid Droplet Theory

The neutron was now recognized by scientists as no longer a theoretical particle but as an actual component of nature. A year after Chadwick announced his discovery, Leo Szilard proposed his theory suggesting that accelerating neutrons could spark the fission reaction. And in 1936 the Danish physicist Niels Bohr proposed a new theory suggesting how the neutron from one atom's nucleus could be captured by the nuclei of other atoms.

Bohr called his idea the liquid droplet theory. He suggested that a mass of atoms behave like a drop of liquid—clustering around one another to form the drop. When bombarded by a neutron, the drop forms the shape of a dumbbell and then splits into two, forming two new drops. During the split into two drops, energy is released. Bohr's theory provided scientists with a visualization of how the actual process of fission would be achieved.

Each of these advancements added new and important layers of understanding to how fission would work once scientists found a way to create chain reactions in their laboratories. Indeed, the era was marked by significant achievements but also significant sadness. In 1934 Marie Curie died at the age of sixty-six. The cause of death was aplastic anemia—the loss of blood cells in her bone marrow. The disease was caused by her constant exposure to radiation. For years, as Curie worked in her lab she took no precautions to shield herself from the radiation that emanated from uranium and other volatile elements she examined. At the time, the health effects of exposure to radioactive materials were not known.

Yet even Curie's death would provide scientists with a greater understanding of the fission reaction. This residual effect of exposure to radiation would become another reason the atomic bomb could be regarded as so deadly. Not only would it create a huge explosion, leveling an entire city, but its effects would last for years afterward. Those who were not killed by the initial explosion nevertheless were exposed to the radiation from the blast and invariably would develop cancer or other ills.

Fission in the Laboratory

The work produced by Curie, Einstein, Rutherford, Cockcroft, Walton, Lawrence, Chadwick, Bohr, and other scientists came to fruition on December 22, 1938, when two German chemists—Otto Hahn and Fritz Strassmann—conducted an experiment providing evidence that the release of energy from the atom was more than a theoretical exercise. Hahn and Strassmann bombarded uranium atoms with neutrons, which caused the uranium to fission—to break up and emit other neutrons. The work of Hahn and Strassmann confirmed the chain reactions that are necessary to release energy from atoms.

They had not been able to control the chain reaction, but Hahn and Strassmann showed that a chain reaction could occur and that, in theory, fission could produce an enormous amount of energy. Hahn and Strassmann suggested that the fission of a single nucleus of uranium could spark a chain reaction releasing energy equivalent to hundreds of millions of electrical volts. "An entirely new class of super-weapon

British scientist James Chadwick constructed a device (pictured) that helped him confirm a third component of atoms—neutrons. Unlike electrons, which carry a negative charge, and protons, which carry a positive charge, neutrons contain no electrical charge.

might be possible, millions of times more destructive than dynamite or TNT," says historian and nuclear scientist Stephen M. Younger. "The largest conventional bomb contained a couple thousand pounds of explosive, but preliminary calculations suggested that even a small atomic bomb would produce thousands of tons of explosive equivalent."[8]

Hitler Comes to Power

The fact that Hahn and Strassmann were pursuing their research in Germany troubled many members of the scientific community in America and western Europe. Indeed, during the 1930s, as scientists broke new ground in atomic physics, events were transpiring in Europe and Asia that would have a profound effect on the course of their research. In 1933 Adolf Hitler became chancellor of Germany and would soon assume the powers of a dictator.

Hitler had been a founder of the National Socialism (Nazi)

movement in Germany. Following the defeat of Germany in World War I—then known as the Great War—Germans fell into a long period of economic depression as their country was forced to pay billions of dollars in reparations to the victors under the terms of the Treaty of Versailles, which ended the war. The Nazis seized power after a tumultuous era in Germany, promising to rebuild the country's military and industry and restore Germany to a preeminent place among the European powers. In fact, the Nazis intended to dominate Europe, invading and enslaving their neighbors while cleansing European society of so-called undesirables: Jews, Slavs, Communists, gays, intellectuals, and virtually anyone else who rose in opposition to their racist policies.

The anti-Semitism that was coming to dominate society in Germany and other European countries forced many top scientists to flee to America and Great Britain. Einstein and Szilard both left Germany in 1933. As other Jewish scientists sought to escape Germany, the Nazi regime issued an order prohibiting the emigration of academics. Meanwhile, under the regime's Nuremberg laws, adopted by the Nazis in 1935, Jews were stripped of their rights of citizenship. This meant that Jews were denied employment, housing, and social services provided by the government—yet they were prohibited from leaving Germany. Eventually Jews and others regarded as undesirable by the Nazis would be rounded up and imprisoned in concentration camps.

One Jewish scientist who at first managed to escape detection by the Nazis was Lise Meitner, a member of the team of scientists working alongside Hahn and Strassmann in the months preceding history's first successful fission experiment. In fact, in the years following the successful achievement of fission, many scientists have suggested that Meitner's work was so important to the experiment that she should share equally in the recognition that has been granted to Hahn and Strassmann.

By the time Hahn and Strassmann produced a fission reaction, though, Meitner had already fled Germany. By then the Nazis were closing in on all Jews living in Germany. Six months before the fission experiment, Meitner—with the help of the Dutch underground—was able to slip into the Netherlands. She eventually found safety in Stockholm, Sweden, where she was provided a position at the Swedish Academy of

The Indestructible Atom

The theory proposed by Democritus—that the atom is indestructible—dominated science for centuries until Albert Einstein published his equation in 1905, suggesting mass could be converted into energy. Until then the world's most prominent scientists all insisted the atom could not be broken apart. "All things considered," Isaac Newton wrote in 1704, "it seems probable to me that God in the beginning formed matter in solid, massy, hard, impenetrable, moveable particles [and] these primitive particles, being solids, are incomparably harder than any porous bodies compounded of them; even so very hard, as never to wear or break into pieces."

Centuries earlier, Greek philosophers had concocted rationalizations for the structure of atoms—all of which had little basis in science. They correctly deduced, for example, that atoms of iron were dense and strong, but they suggested that these tiny particles were equipped with hooks that helped give them strength to bind together. Among their other observations: Water was made up of atoms as well, but water atoms were smooth and slippery. Salt was made up of atoms that tasted like salt—and because the taste of salt could be sharp, salt atoms must surely have pointy ends.

According to science historians Jeremy I. Pfeffer and Shlomo Nir, these theories were able to dominate science for centuries because the study of the elements fell into the hands of alchemists—pseudoscientists who searched for the means to turn elements into precious metals. As Pfeffer and Nir write, "Atoms were forgotten in the frenzy of the alchemists' search."

Jeremy I. Pfeffer and Shlomo Nir, *Modern Physics: An Introductory Text.* London: Imperial College Press, 2013, pp. 226, 225.

Sciences. Even in exile, however, Meitner continued to correspond with Hahn and Strassmann. It was Meitner, along with her nephew, physicist Otto Frisch (who fled the Nazis in 1933), who urged Hahn and Strassmann to employ uranium in the experiment. Meitner and Frisch found that, as a heavy element, the electrical force holding the uranium atom together is stronger than the electrical force attempting to pull it apart. But Meitner and Frisch found that bombarding the uranium atom with an extra neutron changes the chemical composition of the uranium atom—literally causing chaos—forcing the uranium atom to split apart.

The Brink of Warfare

The science pursued by Hahn and Strassmann, with the assistance of Meitner, continued as Hitler consolidated his power and embarked on his quest for expansion, seizing territories Germany had lost under the Treaty of Versailles. In 1938 Germany annexed Austria as well as a German-speaking territory of Czechoslovakia known as the Sudetenland. By 1939 Hitler was making plans to take over the entire country of Czechoslovakia and was also eyeing an invasion of Poland, bringing the European continent to the brink of warfare. Meanwhile, Japan had been taken over by a military-led oligarchy that was pursuing expansionist plans that paralleled those of Hitler in Europe. By the late 1930s the Japanese had attacked and occupied most of China. The Japanese pursued militarization and industrialization with the same fervor as the Germans and were believed now to be poised to attack other Asian countries.

Western political leaders kept a wary eye on the German and Japanese governments, but they were far less knowledgeable about the implications the research conducted by Hahn and Strassmann would have on world events. Several scientists feared the German government could employ the research of Strassmann and Hahn into a bomb-making program, giving Hitler—and his eventual allies, the Japanese—a weapon of mass destruction to use against their enemies. Soon after the Hahn-Strassmann experiment, French physicist Paul Langevin said, "If it gets into the wrong hands, the [neutron] can do the world a good deal more damage than that fool [Hitler] who will sooner or later go to the dogs."[9]

A Letter from Einstein

Another scientist who was well aware of the research under way in Germany was Szilard. In 1938 he had left London to accept a position at Columbia University in New York City. In 1939, after learning that Hahn and Strassmann had achieved fission, Szilard realized what could occur should the Nazis put that research to use in developing a weapon. "All the things which H.G. Wells predicted appeared suddenly real to me,"[10] he said.

Like Szilard, Einstein also had joined the faculty of an American university—in this case, Princeton University in New Jersey. In July 1939 Einstein was spending the summer on Long Island, New York, when he was visited by Szilard and Eugene Wigner, another Hungarian-born physicist who fled the Nazis two years earlier. Although Einstein's equation about the conversion of mass to energy provided the theoretical timber that fueled much of atomic research, Einstein played no role in further research into atomic nuclei or fission reactions. Nevertheless, Szilard and Wigner appealed to Einstein because he was, at the time, the premier scientist living in America. They knew it would take a scientist of Einstein's stature to alert American political leaders to the dangers posed by the fission research under way in Nazi Germany.

Szilard and Wigner spent hours with Einstein, explaining the state of the research and, in particular, the advancement achieved by Hahn and Strassmann in Germany. According to Szilard, Einstein was truly astonished at the degree to which the research had advanced since he had published his equation thirty-four years earlier. Told that Hahn and Strassmann had achieved a chain reaction, Einstein remarked, "I never thought of that!"[11] It did not take long for Szilard and Wigner to convince Einstein of the ramifications should the work of Hahn and Strassmann be further developed: Germany could eventually develop an atomic bomb.

Soon a fourth scientist was invited into the discussion—the Hungarian-born physicist Edward Teller, whose work had also focused on fission. Later the four scientists met with Alexander Sachs, a Russian-born economist who was a friend of President Roosevelt. They decided that Einstein would draft a letter to Roosevelt alerting the president of the danger, and Sachs would deliver it.

Many top Jewish scientists fled Nazi Germany before Adolf Hitler's regime issued an order prohibiting academics from leaving the country. Research by some of these scientists contributed to the eventual development of the bomb.

On September 1, 1939, the German army invaded Poland, touching off World War II—although America's entry into the war was still more than two years in the future. On October 11, Sachs met with Roosevelt and personally handed him the letter drafted by Einstein. In the letter, Einstein briefly summarized the state of research into fission:

> It may become possible to set up a nuclear chain reaction in a large mass of uranium, by which vast amounts of power and

large quantities of new . . . elements would be generated. Now it appears almost certain that this could be achieved in the immediate future. This new phenomenon would also lead to the construction of bombs, and it is conceivable—though much less certain—that extremely powerful bombs of a new type may thus be constructed. A single bomb of this type, carried by boat and exploded in a port, might very well destroy the whole port together with some of the surrounding territory.[12]

The Advisory Committee on Uranium

Einstein also pointed out that various American scientists were engaged in atomic fission research, and he suggested Roosevelt establish a government program to coordinate their work as well as provide funding. Roosevelt told Sachs he would like to take the evening to think it over, and he asked Sachs to return the next day for a second meeting.

The next morning Roosevelt met with Sachs and US Army general Edwin "Pa" Wilson, a chief military aide to the president. Roosevelt said he was convinced that if Hitler obtained an atomic bomb, the Nazi dictator would not hesitate to use it on European cities. Turning to Wilson, Roosevelt said, "Pa, this requires action."[13] Ten days later Wilson convened the first meeting of the Advisory Committee on Uranium.

The meeting marked a humble beginning for the US atomic weapons program. The committee, which was chaired by Wilson, at first offered a mere $6,000 to assist in fission research. But as Hitler's armies achieved victories over European nations and millions of Jews, Slavs, and others were enslaved or exterminated in concentration camps, it became clear to Roosevelt that the atomic bomb should become a research priority, and a significant project should be launched with the goal of beating the Germans, and the Japanese, to the bomb.

Chapter 2

The Chicago Pile

America's program to develop the atomic bomb would soon grow into a much larger effort than the Advisory Committee on Uranium had sparked with its initial grant of $6,000. In 1940, as war raged in Europe, Roosevelt grew increasingly convinced that America would be drawn into the conflict. He asked Congress to increase spending on conventional weapons, but he also knew science would play an important role in the outcome of the war.

In June 1940 Roosevelt created the National Defense Research Committee. The agency was tasked with monitoring all areas of scientific study believed to have military use should America be drawn into World War II. Roosevelt appointed engineer Vannevar Bush to head the committee. Soon after taking the job, Bush reviewed the progress of atomic research and confirmed Einstein's belief that a devastating weapon could be created through the achievement of fission. Uranium, Bush told Roosevelt in a memo, "will apparently be more powerful than we thought, the amount necessary seems to be less, the possibilities of actual production appear more certain."[14]

America entered the war in December 1941 following the Japanese attack on the US Navy base at Pearl Harbor in Hawaii. Just four months later Congress appropriated $133 million to fund fission research. Eventually the project would grow beyond that amount, and by the time the atomic bomb was developed, some $20 billion would be spent on its creation. In addition, more than 130,000 people would play a role in the bomb's development.

The effort to develop the atomic bomb was dubbed the Manhattan Project because initially facilities for the project were spread across ten locations in the New York City borough. These facilities included warehouses, laboratories, and the headquarters for the project, located in an office on the eighteenth floor of a Lower Manhattan skyscraper.

The project's official name was the Manhattan Engineer District, although it soon became known simply as the Manhattan Project. The name was selected by US Army general Leslie Groves, who was appointed to head the project. Knowing the bomb had to be developed in complete secrecy, Groves wanted a nondescript, bureaucratic name for the project so that it would not draw attention. "He was nuts about not attracting attention,"[15] says historian Robert S. Norris.

The USS West Virginia *and the USS* Tennessee *burn during the December 1941 Japanese attack on Pearl Harbor. The attack drew the United States into World War II and set in motion congressional funding for fission research.*

Groves was selected to head the Manhattan Project in September 1942. Military officials placed him in charge of the project because of his reputation as a no-nonsense officer who could get things done. Groves was assigned to the US Army Corps of Engineers, the construction division of the army. In his previous assignment he had headed construction of the Pentagon, the massive building in Washington, DC, that serves as headquarters of the American military.

Groves wasted no time. Immediately after accepting the job, he placed an aide, Colonel Keith Nichols, in charge of procuring uranium. In a short time every available pound of uranium—which is obtained through mining—was bought up by the Manhattan Project at a cost of a dollar a pound. Eventually the Manhattan Project's supply of uranium grew to a cache of some 2.5 million pounds (1.1 million kg).

Although the development of the atomic bomb would be a military project, Groves realized it would rely mostly on the talents of civilian scientists. This meant he would need to appoint a civilian director who could deftly coordinate the many facets of fission research. Groves asked physicist J. Robert Oppenheimer to take on that role.

Oppenheimer Joins the Project

Born into a wealthy New York City family in 1904, Oppenheimer discovered science at the age of five when his parents took him to Germany to meet his grandparents. During the visit Oppenheimer's grandfather gave him a rock collection. The boy took the rock collection home and spent hours searching New York parks for unique specimens of rocks, which he added to the collection. Soon the Oppenheimers' fashionable New York apartment was lined with shelves bearing specimens from Oppenheimer's rock collection. While still a child, his parents gave him his first microscope.

In 1921 Oppenheimer was named valedictorian of his high school graduating class and planned to enter Harvard University. Shortly before entering college, however, he was stricken with appendicitis. Too ill to enter Harvard, Oppenheimer spent months recovering from the operation that removed his appendix. In late 1921 Oppenheimer's

The Vision of Vannevar Bush

As head of the National Defense Research Committee, Vannevar Bush advised president Franklin D. Roosevelt to pursue development of the atomic bomb. Following World War II, Bush suggested that science pursue another device that would have an enormous impact on life in the twenty-first century: the personal computer.

Writing in *Atlantic* magazine in 1945, Bush called on scientists and engineers to devote their skills to a device that would sit on a desktop and place at the fingertips of users huge quantities of data. Bush called the device the memex, describing it as a machine in which an "individual stores all his books, records, and communications, and which is mechanized so that it may be consulted with exceeding speed and flexibility."

At the time Bush conceived of the device, only a handful of computers were in operation, and these machines typically cost millions of dollars and were housed on entire floors of buildings. Still, Bush found no reason why computers could not be miniaturized and made available to individuals. In his description of the device, he came remarkably close to how personal computers would eventually be designed some thirty years later. He wrote, "It consists of a desk, and while it can be operated from a distance, it is primarily the piece of furniture at which [the user] works. On top are slanting translucent screens, on which material can be projected for convenient reading. There is a keyboard, and sets of buttons and levers. Otherwise, it looks like an ordinary desk."

Quoted in James G. Rice, "The Dream of the Memex," *American Libraries*, January 1988, p. 14.

father sent him to New Mexico to regain his strength by riding horses and hiking the desert trails. Oppenheimer fell in love with New Mexico and in later years leased a ranch in the Sangre de Cristo Mountains, where he would often spend weeks on horseback, riding and camping far into the countryside.

Fully recovered from the surgery, Oppenheimer entered Harvard in 1922. He initially majored in chemistry, but a year later he changed his major to physics. He graduated in three years, first in his class, and then enrolled in the University of Göttingen in Germany to pursue his doctoral degree. His doctoral thesis, written in 1927, focused on the physical properties of the atom.

Returning to the United States, Oppenheimer taught at Harvard and the California Institute of Technology and pursued research in a number of fields in physics. He was the first to predict the existence of black holes, stars so dense that even light cannot escape their forces of gravity. But atomic physics remained his true interest, and he encouraged many of his students to pursue the study of fission. Oppenheimer's own 1942 research was focused on critical mass—the amount of fissionable material required to spark a chain reaction—when he was asked to join the Manhattan Project as a research scientist.

When Groves joined the Manhattan Project, he knew virtually nothing about physics. He found Oppenheimer to be an amiable teacher, enduring the general's constant questions about fission and similar matters that the other scientists refused to make time to answer. Oppenheimer won Groves's respect, and so when Groves concluded that he would need a civilian scientist to oversee the entire project, he asked Oppenheimer to accept the job. "Why, Oppenheimer knows everything," Groves said after the war. "He can talk to you about anything you bring up. Well, not exactly. I guess there are a few things he doesn't know about. He doesn't know anything about sports."[16]

Oppenheimer's Intensity

In his role as civilian director of the project, Oppenheimer—known to his colleagues as "Oppie"—pursued no research on his own. Instead, he familiarized himself with the many individual research projects under way and traveled constantly, sitting in on experiments and briefings and adding his expertise to the conversation.

A Belgian's Contribution to the Manhattan Project

Most of the uranium produced for the Manhattan Project was mined in Katanga, a region in Africa in what is now the Democratic Republic of the Congo but in the 1940s was part of a colony under the control of Belgium. Since Belgium fell under the occupation of the Nazis in May 1940, the Manhattan Project had to find a way to obtain the Katanga uranium in secret. Officials soon made contact with Edgar Sengier, the head of the Belgian mining company Union Minière du Haut Katanga.

Sengier escaped the Nazi occupation, and by 1942 he was living in New York. Before fleeing Belgium, Sengier had ordered his company's uranium mine in Katanga sealed, fearing what could occur should the mineral fall into the hands of the Nazis. Contacted by Colonel Keith Nichols, an aide to General Groves, Sengier arranged for the shipment of 1,250 tons (1,134 metric tons) of uranium from the Shinkolobwe mine in Katanga to the United States.

Quietly, Sengier had the mine reopened and the uranium loaded into barrels and carried by railway to the African port city of Lobito. The barrels were then shipped across the Atlantic on two freighters. Sengier had the uranium stored in a vegetable oil warehouse in Staten Island, New York. To prevent warehouse workers from opening what they would naturally assume to be barrels containing vegetable oil, Sengier had each barrel stamped with the words *Uranium Ore—Product of the Belgian Congo.* Following the war, to recognize his contribution to the Manhattan Project, Congress awarded Sengier the Medal of Merit, a civilian honor.

Because Groves insisted on secrecy, many scientists were unaware of the nature of the research pursued by their colleagues. This could hamper their own work since discoveries made by some scientists were not shared with others. But by reviewing everyone's work, Oppenheimer was often able to help fill in the gaps, advising the scientists that the questions they were trying to answer had already been tackled in other laboratories.

"Everyone sensed Oppie's presence," report historians Kai Bird and Martin J. Sherwin. "He drove himself around . . . in an Army jeep or his own large black Buick, dropping in unannounced on one of the [project's] scattered offices. Usually he'd sit in the back of the room, chain-smoking and listening quietly to the discussion. His mere presence seemed to galvanize people to greater efforts."[17] And Manhattan Project physicist Victor Weisskopf recalled, "He was present in the laboratory or in the seminar rooms when a new effect was measured, when a new idea was conceived. It was not that he contributed so many ideas or suggestions; he did so, sometimes, but his main influence came from something else. It was his continuous and intense presence, which produced a direct sense of participation in all of us."[18]

Controlling Fission

It was soon clear to Oppenheimer and Groves that the project would need larger and better-equipped facilities than were available in New York City. They traveled across the country scouting locations for laboratories and other facilities that could be used by the Manhattan Project scientists. One such laboratory was found at the University of Chicago, where an early and decisive scientific achievement was realized in late 1942. A team of scientists under the direction of Italian-born physicist Enrico Fermi had been recruited to build on the research of Hahn and Strassmann with the goal of not only sparking a fission reaction in the laboratory but controlling it as well.

Indeed, the key to developing an atomic bomb rested in the ability to control the chain reaction. In other words, the bomb maker must have the ability to spark the separation of the neutrons and initiate the fission reaction at a prescribed moment. (If a bomb is dropped from an airplane over an enemy city, the bomb must ignite at a precise moment in order for it to be effective.) That was the purpose of the experiment

American physicist J. Robert Oppenheimer (pictured) served as civilian director of the Manhattan Project. In that role he brought continuity to the many research projects under way.

that brought the Manhattan Project scientists together under the stands of Stagg Field, the University of Chicago's football stadium, on December 2, 1942.

The Fermis Flee Italy

The more than fifty Manhattan Project scientists and engineers who carried out the experiment worked under the leadership of Fermi, who had won the 1938 Nobel Prize in Physics for his work in pioneering the science of fission reactions. In his Nobel-winning experiment Fermi concluded that if neutrons were slowed during fission through the use of sheathing processes, new forms of existing elements, known as isotopes, could be created as new nuclei are formed. Later, this research would be employed by the Manhattan Project to refine uranium into a specific isotope with destructive qualities.

Fermi and his wife, Laura, fled to America from the dictatorship of Benito Mussolini. Under Mussolini, the Italian government had adopted the racist and anti-Semitic principles of the Nazis and would ally with the Germans and Japanese in the war. Fermi found he could not live under Mussolini's Fascist regime; moreover, despite his prominence in the Italian scientific community, Fermi knew the life of his wife, who was Jewish, was in peril. In 1938 the couple traveled to Sweden so that Fermi could accept the Nobel Prize. Instead of returning to Italy following the ceremony, they fled to Great Britain and eventually America, where Fermi accepted a teaching position at Columbia University. While teaching at Columbia, he was invited to join the Manhattan Project.

The experiment headed by Fermi attempted to stage the first controlled chain reaction. To produce the reaction, the Manhattan Project took over an indoor squash court located under the Stagg Field stands, where the scientists constructed what they called Chicago Pile Number One (CP-1). CP-1 consisted of some 46 tons (42 metric tons) of uranium.

Building the Pile

Uranium's highly volatile properties suggested to Fermi that neutrons in the uranium atom could be prompted to separate from their nuclei. However, because uranium can emit neutrons, it is very unstable. And so the Manhattan Project scientists enclosed the uranium in a mass of bricks made out of graphite—some 380 tons (345 metric tons) had to be employed. The graphite absorbed the uranium neutrons to a degree, essentially slowing them down. When it was ready for the experiment, the CP-1 stood some 26 feet (8 m) high.

To produce the chain reaction, the scientists planned to remove rods from the pile composed of the element cadmium. The cadmium rods were inserted into the pile to absorb the free-flying uranium neutrons. As the cadmium rods were removed, the neutrons would strike the uranium nuclei, sparking chain reactions. "An atomic chain reaction may be compared to the burning of a rubbish pile from spontaneous combustion," explained Fermi. "In such a fire, minute parts of the pile start to burn and in turn ignite other tiny fragments. When sufficient numbers of these fractional parts are heated to the kindling points, the entire heap bursts into flames."[19]

By controlling the rods, the Manhattan Project scientists would have the ability to control the chain reactions. As the rods were removed from the pile, more chain reactions would occur. Moreover, as the rods were pulled out, instruments would record the level of radioactivity—the release of neutrons. These instruments, known as Geiger counters—named for the device's coinventor, German physicist Johannes Geiger—had been developed in 1928 and were capable of measuring radioactivity by making clacking sounds. The more clacks, the more radioactivity was present. Similar instruments recorded the radioactivity on charts, showing spikes as the chain reactions occurred.

An Element of Danger

There was an element of danger to the experiment. Since scientists had never before attempted to control a chain reaction, it was possible the reactions would be sparked beyond their means to control them. Given the volatility of the uranium, an explosion was certainly possible. To guard against an out-of-control reaction, three scientists held pails of liquid cadmium that they were instructed to pour on the pile should the reactions rage out of control.

It was the job of George Weil to remove the rods. Weil was a young scientist who worked under Fermi at Columbia. Weil and the other participants spent much of the day conducting preliminary tests of the equipment. All went well, and at 3:25 p.m. Fermi gave the order to withdraw the first cadmium rod. Weil withdrew the rod slowly, moving the rod just 6 inches (15 cm) at a time. With every pull, the Geiger

The Geiger counter (pictured), developed by German physicist Johannes Geiger, measured levels of radioactivity by making clacking sounds. The more clacks, the more radioactivity was present.

counters came to life. Recalled another scientist, Herbert Anderson, "At first you could hear the sound of the [Geiger] counter, clickety-clack, clickety-clack. Then the clicks came more and more rapidly, and after a while they began to merge into a roar: the counter couldn't follow anymore."[20] Similarly, the instruments recording the radioactivity on paper were also going wild, drawing huge peaks as the cadmium rods were withdrawn. At 3:53 p.m. Fermi instructed Weil to reinsert the rods. Within seconds, the instruments grew silent.

Everyone in the room knew the significance of the moment. The amount of energy released by the experiment was negligible; Fermi later said the uranium had barely given off enough energy to illuminate a single lightbulb. But for twenty-eight minutes the Manhattan Project scientists were able to control an atomic chain reaction.

Oak Ridge

One reason the Chicago Pile had given off so little energy was due to the quality of the uranium used during the test. In the University of Chicago test the Manhattan Project scientists used uranium in its natural state. Although certainly volatile, uranium found in its natural form is still too stable an element to be of much use in a bomb. But because uranium emits neutrons, its chemical composition can—as Fermi proved—be converted into new versions of itself. These new versions are known as isotopes. The uranium isotope known as U-235 is highly volatile and, unlike the raw version of uranium, capable of producing a massive amount of energy during a fission reaction. Therefore, to spark a chain reaction with the destructive force required for an atomic weapon, the Manhattan Project scientists needed to find a way to convert—or enrich—uranium, turning it into the isotope U-235.

For that research, Groves and Oppenheimer established a lab at Oak Ridge, Tennessee. Although a number of Manhattan Project labs tackled the uranium-enrichment process, most of the work was performed at Oak Ridge. Oak Ridge was, in fact, not even a town prior to the Manhattan Project. The federal government acquired 60,000 acres (24,281 ha) along the Clinch River in eastern Tennessee in 1942 and paid for the creation of the laboratory and production facilities as well as housing for the scientists, production workers, and their families. The uranium-enrichment program at Oak Ridge required the construction of 268 separate buildings. By 1945 Oak Ridge was the size of a small city, with roughly one hundred thousand residents—with the majority of the adult population employed in production of enriched uranium. As historian Gerard J. DeGroot writes, "Oak Ridge is testimony to the ingenuity and determination of wartime America. The plant was constructed from scratch in less than a year."[21]

Enriching Uranium

The Oak Ridge scientists experimented with a number of methods to convert ordinary uranium into U-235. One method they tried was to spin the uranium at a high rate of speed in a device known as a centrifuge. By doing so, it was hoped the molecules composing U-235 would separate; however, the Oak Ridge scientists learned they could not spin the uranium fast enough to effectively separate the lighter U-235 molecules.

They had much more success with processes that employed electromagnetism and gas diffusion. In the electromagnetic process, scientists would separate the U-235 isotope from uranium by employing gargantuan magnets. Engineers overseeing construction of the magnets soon encountered a major problem: The magnets required huge quantities of copper wire, which was in short supply. (Due to the war many raw materials, such as copper, were in short supply because they were diverted to the manufacture of conventional arms.) Instead of using copper, the Manhattan Project engineers found they could build the magnets by employing silver wire, and they found an abundant supply of the precious metal in the vaults of the US Treasury Department. Eventually the Treasury made 13,500 tons (12,247 metric tons) of silver available to the Manhattan Project.

The process suffered from other setbacks. Work on the magnets commenced in February 1943, but the design contained numerous flaws, which interrupted the electrical current supplying the magnetic force. The Manhattan Project scientists had hoped to have use of forty-eight magnets to enrich uranium, but technical difficulties hampered progress and the magnets were not ready for testing until early 1944.

Even so, the magnets were tremendous engineering achievements. Each magnet weighed between 3,000 and 10,000 tons (2,722 and 9,072 metric tons) and used as much electrical power as a city. When the magnets came to life, anyone in the vicinity of the devices could feel their pull—they were strong enough to tug on women's hairpins.

Meanwhile, other Manhattan Project scientists were enriching uranium through the thermal-diffusion process. By heating a thin, vertically held film of uranium on one side and cooling it on the other, they were able to draw the U-235 molecules to the top of the film.

This project required the construction of thousands of tanks that would contain the uranium. The tanks were erected in a single building at Oak Ridge that stood four stories high, 1,000 feet (305 m) wide, and 0.5 miles (0.8 km) in length. Some twelve thousand people worked in the thermal diffusion building. If dirt found its way into the tanks, the uranium would be fouled; therefore, the building had to be kept spotless—a tremendous task given that twelve thousand people were constantly entering and leaving the building. Establishing the facilities for thermal-diffusion production proved to be an enormous engineering challenge, and not until early 1945 would Oak Ridge start producing weapons-grade U-235.

The projects to control fission and produce weapons-grade uranium illustrate the challenges facing the Manhattan Project scientists as they pursued development of the atomic bomb. Indeed, the establishment of the huge facility at Oak Ridge illustrates the virtually unlimited resources the US government placed in the hands of Groves and Oppenheimer, burdening these two leaders with the awesome responsibility of developing a weapon that could assure victory for the Allies.

Chapter 3

Site Y

The University of Chicago and the new town of Oak Ridge, Tennessee, were just two of the many locations spread across America where research and development of the atomic bomb were under way. Scientists, engineers, and others could be found toiling in such locations as Ames, Iowa, where uranium enrichment was also performed; Uravan, Colorado, where the federal government financed a uranium mine; and Inyokern, California, where engineering work was conducted on finding an effective way to detonate the bomb. In three American towns—Morgantown, West Virginia; Newport, Indiana; and Sylacauga, Alabama—factories had been erected to produce a substance known as heavy water.

Ordinary water is composed of two atoms of hydrogen and one atom of oxygen—the chemical symbol is H_2O. Heavy water contains a form of hydrogen known as deuterium—its chemical symbol is D_2O. Deuterium differs from hydrogen in that it contains an extra neutron. The extra neutron makes the deuterium weigh more than ordinary hydrogen; hence the name *heavy water*. Scientists found that when they doused U-235 with heavy water, they were able to stabilize the isotope's neutrons and therefore slow the chain reaction—giving them more control over fission.

Spreading the Manhattan Project across the country suited General Groves. He was obsessed with secrecy. He believed that to maintain security the work should be conducted in many locations, thus preventing foreign spies from gaining access to the whole project through any single facility. Moreover, he believed security could best be maintained if the workers did not even know the purpose of their jobs. The heavy water–production workers knew, for example, they were producing the substance, but they did not know what use was intended for the water. Only a handful of the most senior officials and scientists were aware of the true purpose of their work. "For Groves, secrecy was paramount," says historian DeGroot. "He wanted scientists to be restricted from speaking to each other and kept ignorant of progress outside their own lab. Only a select few would be familiar with the entire project; most would not even know what they were making."[22]

Los Alamos

Oppenheimer agreed with the importance of maintaining secrecy and security but feared Groves's obsession with secrecy was slowing progress. As a scientist, Oppenheimer knew science is often enhanced through the free flow of ideas—and by visiting the various laboratories on his own, he did what he could to keep his colleagues informed about each other's research. Nevertheless, Oppenheimer wanted the Manhattan Project scientists to be able to discuss their work with one another, compare notes, and offer solutions to problems by bringing fresh perspectives to their conversations.

Finally, he suggested to Groves that the Manhattan Project establish one central laboratory where the project's top scientists could be brought together to work as a team. It would be a place, Oppenheimer suggested, "where people could talk freely to each other, where theoretical ideas and experimental findings could affect each other, where the waste and frustration and error of the many compartmentalized experimental studies could be eliminated."[23] Groves agreed but placed a stipulation on the plan: The central laboratory must be isolated, located miles away from civilization so the military could maintain a tight degree of security over the research. Also, due to the volatile nature of the research, Groves believed that in the event of an accidental explosion, an isolated location would offer the best protection against widespread damage and loss of life. Groves was concerned about an accidental atomic explosion occurring at a lab located in a big city.

Oppenheimer accepted Groves's conditions and immediately suggested an isolated part of New Mexico where he had spent summers as

Manhattan Project Research and Production Sites

a boy. After some scouting, Oppenheimer found a private boys' school, the Los Alamos Ranch School, that offered many amenities the Manhattan Project would need. In addition to its remote location, dormitories and dining facilities were already in place. The federal government bought the school from its owners for $440,000—a sum the owners were more than happy to accept, given that enrollment had fallen off and the school was facing hard times. The few remaining students were told to find new schools, and in 1943 the Army Corps of Engineers arrived to build laboratories, additional housing, and to satisfy Groves, a chain-link fence—topped with three layers of barbed wire—around the whole complex. Indeed, Groves, who was still obsessed with security, concocted a cover story that suggested the facility was a research center owned by the University of California. Moreover, in official government communications, the newly launched Los Alamos National Laboratory was referred to as Site Y.

Desert Life

Oppenheimer originally envisioned Los Alamos housing thirty scientists and their families. In fact, Groves wanted to confine everybody to the facility within the chain-link fence and even issue military-style uniforms to the scientists. But the scientists balked; they wanted to bring their families, they did not want to live in what was essentially a barracks, and they certainly did not want to wear uniforms. And so, as in the case of Oak Ridge, a new town would be erected near the lab to accommodate the Los Alamos workers and their families. By 1945 the town of Los Alamos had grown to a population of some six thousand people, virtually all of whom had some connection to the work at the laboratory.

And despite Groves's insistence on secrecy, it was clear to many people who lived in the American Southwest that something important was going on in New Mexico. For months scientists and their families made their way to New Mexico—many by train, others by car. Ruth Marshak, the wife of physicist Robert Marshak, recalls driving cross-country to New Mexico in 1943 and stopping for gasoline in Colorado, just short of the New Mexico border. "The attendant looked over the loaded car, examined our license plates, and asked us where we were heading," she recalled. "We replied that we were bound for New Mexico. The man studied my husband and said, 'Oh, you folks must be going to that secret project!'"[24]

The Marshaks, as well as everyone else heading for Los Alamos, first met with Oppenheimer's assistant, Dorothy McKibbin, whose office was in Santa Fe, the New Mexico city about 35 miles (56 km) southeast of Los Alamos. McKibbin's job was to find housing for the scientists and their families and see to their needs. Throughout the course of the Manhattan Project, she proved to be an invaluable member of Oppenheimer's team, serving as a conduit between the scientists and the outside world.

Barracks-style huts (pictured) provided housing for the first scientists and their families to arrive at Los Alamos National Laboratory in New Mexico. Eventually a new town was erected to accommodate the growing population of workers and family members.

Many of the new residents of Los Alamos were European immigrants. At one time residents of such cosmopolitan European cities as Berlin, Vienna, and Prague, they had escaped the Nazi regime to work on the side of the Allies. Yet now they found themselves laboring in the dusty New Mexico desert. Fermi and Teller relocated to Los Alamos, but Szilard refused, preferring to continue working at the University of Chicago. "Nobody could think straight in a place like that," Szilard insisted. "Everybody who goes there will go crazy."[25]

Enriching Plutonium

Still, though, the federal government found no shortage of scientists willing to endure the desert climate, spartan living arrangements, military-style security, and low pay for life in Los Alamos. They volunteered out of patriotism, to be sure, but also out of an interest in participating in the most cutting-edge science in the history of the world. Chemist Glenn Seaborg, who recruited many scientists to Los Alamos, told new staff members, "No matter what you do with the rest of your life nothing will be as important to the future of the world as your work on this Project right now."[26]

As the Los Alamos scientists adjusted to life in the desert, they were accomplishing important tasks in their labs. Fermi headed experiments in critical mass—the determination of just how little atomic material would be needed to sustain a chain reaction. It was an important field of research, given that there would be little room in the actual bomb for fissionable material. Meanwhile, physicist Emilio Segrè found the radioactive element plutonium also could be sparked into a chain reaction. Indeed, plutonium was found to emit more neutrons than U-235, meaning it could be possible to use less plutonium than enriched uranium in the bomb.

Based on the work of Segrè and other researchers, Groves and Oppenheimer concluded that they had to establish a plant to enrich plutonium into weapons-grade material. Groves found 500,000 acres (202,343 ha) in a remote corner of Washington State near the town of Hanford. As with Oak Ridge, an enrichment plant was erected in a few short months—some forty-five thousand construction workers were dispatched to Hanford in 1943. By 1945 the Hanford Engineering Works consisted of 554 buildings (not including homes) as well as 64 underground waste storage tanks, 386 miles (621 km) of roads, 158 miles (254 km) of railways, 50 miles (80 km) of electrical lines, and of course, a sturdy fence around the whole compound. The complex sprawled across two counties in Washington: Benton and Franklin. Prior to the arrival of the Manhattan Project, the combined population of the two counties was nineteen thousand people; by 1945 more than seventy thousand people were living in Benton and Franklin counties, and most of them held jobs at the plant that enriched plutonium for the atomic bomb.

The Gadget

As work proceeded on enriching fissionable material at Oak Ridge and Hanford, the actual design of the bomb was beginning to take shape at

Life in Los Alamos

The scientists who lived in Los Alamos during the development of the atomic bomb found a life unlike what they had known in the major American or European cities where they had previously made their homes. For example, bathtubs in Los Alamos were rare. Only the most senior scientists were provided with homes on what was known as Bathtub Row. These homes, which included bathtubs, were located on the main street of Los Alamos and formerly had housed the teachers of the Los Alamos Ranch School.

General Groves was so dedicated to secrecy at the laboratory that he decreed everyone in Los Alamos would share a single mailing address: Post Office Box 16634, Santa Fe, New Mexico. As such, everyone's mail was collected by the military at the Santa Fe post office and then delivered to the laboratory.

From 1943 to 1945 more than two hundred babies were born into the families of Los Alamos scientists—a circumstance that worried Groves, who believed children could compromise security. As a bit of fun, somebody made up a jingle giving voice to the general's concern:

> The General's in a stew
> He trusted you and you
> He thought you'd be scientific
> Instead you're just prolific
> And what is he to do?

Quoted in Cynthia C. Kelly, ed., *The Manhattan Project: The Birth of the Atomic Bomb in the Words of Its Creators, Eyewitnesses, and Historians.* New York: Black Dog & Leventhal, 2007, p. 170.

Los Alamos. A group of scientists headed by Hans Bethe, a German-born physicist, worked with US Navy engineers on designs for the weapon, which the scientists had taken to calling *the gadget*. According to mathematician Paul Olum, "We never called it a bomb, lest somehow the word slip out in some unauthorized place. It was always referred to as the 'gadget.'"[27] The group of scientists working on the design included a staff of metallurgists who were charged with transforming the uranium and plutonium into metals that could be encased in the bomb.

Another team worked on developing cannons designed to actually shoot shells that would detonate into atomic explosions. This technique was known as implosion. In theory, a shell containing a critical mass of uranium or plutonium would be fired at the enemy. En route to the target, a conventional explosion in the shell would detonate, initiating a fission reaction within the atomic material in the shell. The shell would then implode, destroying itself before actually hitting the target. In contrast, a conventional shell explodes as it hits the target.

By 1944, though, work on the cannons was halted. The implosion method was found to be too unstable, and scientists had little control over the chain reaction once the shell left the cannon and was traveling to its target. The research showed a very real danger of the chain reaction commencing before the shell had the chance to implode. With the cannon project killed, work focused entirely on delivering the bomb from an aircraft flying over the target.

Japan's Bomb Program

As work proceeded at Los Alamos and elsewhere in America, Allied intelligence agencies had been following the atomic weapons projects under way in both Germany and Japan. In Japan the project was headed by Yoshio Nishina, who had studied under nuclear physicist Niels Bohr in Denmark and had set up the Riken Institute for Physical and Chemical Research in the Japanese capital of Tokyo. Nishina built two cyclotrons at the Riken Institute. Another key scientist was Ryokichi Sagane, who had studied under Erneset O. Lawrence at the University of California at Berkeley.

The Japanese atomic weapons program was hampered by many problems. For starters, the government could never provide the same level of resources to Nishina and Sagane that the American government provided to Groves and Oppenheimer. With only a handful of laboratories

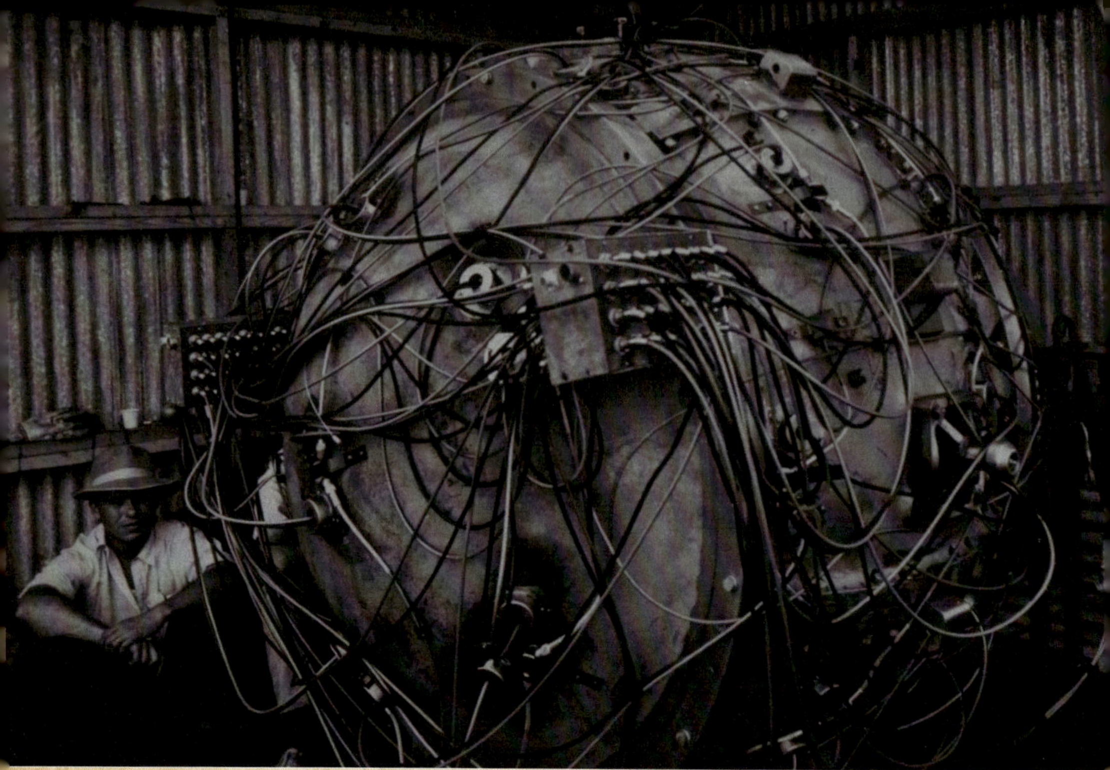

A photograph from the 1940s shows a scientist sitting beside the gadget, *the name scientists on the project gave to the still-secret bomb. They never used the term* bomb, *to avoid unwittingly revealing information about their work.*

and production facilities devoted to atomic research in Japan, work progressed slowly. For example, it took the Japanese scientists eighteen months to successfully enrich their first pile of uranium—a task that was accomplished in America in a matter of weeks. In fact, the Japanese program lacked access to abundant supplies of uranium. Prior to the war the Japanese army occupied the region of China known as Manchuria, where uranium deposits were known to exist. But the Japanese lacked widespread knowledge of mining techniques, which hampered their ability to obtain large quantities of uranium. Bombing raids by Allied forces over Manchuria also slowed Japanese efforts to acquire uranium.

During the early phase of the war, Japan's military leaders placed a low priority on development of the atomic bomb because they were certain they would achieve their objectives with existing weapons. After the surprise attack on Pearl Harbor had crippled America's Pacific-based fleet, Japan easily achieved victories as it attacked and defeated the Americans at Guam and Wake Island and the British at Malaya and Singapore. The Japanese followed that victory by defeating the Allies in the Battle of the Java Sea, then drove General Douglas MacArthur's troops out of the Philippines. Not until 1943, when the US Navy defeated the Japanese at Guadalcanal, would the Pacific War turn in favor of the Allies. In the coming months, Allied troops would move closer to Japan as the Japanese navy lost a significant battle off the coast of Saipan and then suffered another defeat as MacArthur returned to liberate the Philippines. In 1944 the Americans retook Guam.

Nazi Plans Falter

Only as the Japanese continued to suffer military setbacks did the government begin to place importance on its atomic weapons program. The government established the Japan Society for the Promotion of Science, designating several laboratories for weapons research at a number of Japanese universities. The Japanese military also set up a Science Mobilization Council to coordinate weapons research. Thirty two separate weapons programs were funded under the council's control. But infighting within the council slowed research as different programs competed for financial support. Since fission research was just one of the projects pursued, the Japanese atomic bomb program lacked political and financial support. Moreover, some of Japan's most innovative scientists were assigned to other projects, robbing the fission program of the intellectual support that, in the United States, was almost solely focused on development of an atomic weapon.

In Germany the Nazis also commenced an atomic weapons program, but they were largely hampered by a lack of intellectual resources. Many of the best German scientists were either Jews or others who refused to work for the Nazi regime. If they had not already fled to America or Great Britain, it is likely they were imprisoned in concentration camps. Back in 1933, soon after he ascended to power and began purging Jews from German society, Hitler was warned by Max Planck, a German physicist, that the purge could rob Germany of some of the country's best scientific minds. Hitler responded, "Our national policies will not be revoked or modified, even for scientists. If the dismissal of Jewish scientists means the annihilation of contemporary German science, then we shall do without science for a few years!"[28]

Following the Hahn-Strassmann experiment, the German army established an atomic weapons research program led by physicist Kurt Diebner. By 1941 the program had built centrifuges in an attempt to enrich uranium. However, Diebner's research was slowed by the same problem that afflicted his colleagues in Japan: The German government was unable to devote considerable resources to fission research. Supplying the army with conventional weapons placed a financial burden on the German government, leaving the Nazi regime few resources to devote to research on the atomic bomb.

A Commando Raid in Norway

The Germans did convert a water treatment plant in Norway into a heavy water–production facility. The Norsk Hydro plant in Vemork, Norway, would become the scene of one of the most heroic espionage missions of the war. A team of Norwegian commandos staged a daring raid there, crippling the plant and seriously hampering the Nazi atomic weapons program.

The British had been eyeing the Norsk plant for months with plans to stage a raid by sending in commandos on a glider mission. Soon after Groves assumed command of the Manhattan Project, he made inquiries into the German program and learned of the heavy water plant at Vemork. He asked the British to speed up their plans for the raid. On October 18, 1942, four Norwegian commandos parachuted into Vemork as an advance party for the raid, which was scheduled for November 19. When the date of the raid arrived, though, the British gliders ran into bad weather. The two gliders crashed into a mountainside in Norway; fourteen commandos who survived the crash were captured by the Germans.

The Allies tried again on February 16, 1943, sending in six Norwegian commandos; all made successful parachute jumps into the mountains near Vemork. The commandos were all skilled mountaineers and skiers, and they put their talents to use as they climbed and skied

The Second Raid on Vemork

Although the commando raid on Vemork seriously crippled the Nazi heavy water plant in Norway, by late 1943 Allied intelligence agents learned that the plant was once again producing heavy water. A bombing mission was dispatched, and again the plant was crippled by the attack, but spies learned the Nazis managed to shield thirty-nine barrels of heavy water from the bombing. Moreover, the agents learned of plans to ship the water to laboratories in Germany.

Once again Norwegian commando Knut Haukelid was called on to destroy the heavy water. Haukelid conceived a plan to blow up a ferry carrying the barrels as the boat crossed Lake Tinnsjå in Norway. Haukelid was able to plant explosives on the ferry. On February 20, 1944, as the ferry reached the middle of the lake, a timer activated the explosives, blowing a hole in the hull.

The barrels of heavy water rolled into the lake and were lost to the Nazi atomic weapons program. Fifty-three people were also aboard the ferry; twenty-six died in the explosion. Later Kurt Diebner, the head of the Nazi atomic weapons program, attributed the failure of his program mostly to sabotage committed by Haukelid. He said, "It was the elimination of German heavy-water production in Norway that was the main factor in our failure to achieve a self-sustaining atomic [reaction] before the war ended."

Quoted in Richard Rhodes, *The Making of the Atomic Bomb*. New York: Simon & Schuster, 2012, p. 517.

through the mountains while carrying explosives on their backs. Eventually they rendezvoused with the four Norwegians who had entered the region five months earlier.

On the night of February 27, the Norwegian commandos made their way to the Norsk plant. "It was a dark night and there was no moon,"[29] recalled the commando leader, Knut Haukelid. It was very windy, though, a condition which the commandos found to their advantage. The German guards were loath to spend much time outdoors making their rounds, and the sound of the wind drowned out the noise the commandos made tinkering with the explosives.

They cut through a chain-link fence surrounding the plant. Scouts had located a tunnel the Germans had constructed to lay cable into the plant. The commandos crawled through the tunnel, placing explosives at the entrance to the facility where the heavy water was made. In all, the demolition party set eighteen charges at the plant. As the commandos slipped away, they ignited the charges. The first sound Haukelid heard was what he believed to be an insignificant pop, and he worried that the charges had failed. "Was this what we had come over a thousand miles to do?"[30] he wondered. A few minutes later, though, huge explosions ripped through the plant.

The explosions destroyed the entire stock of heavy water at Norsk and seriously crippled the production facility. It would take nearly a year for German engineers to repair the damage caused by the raid. By then it was late 1943. The Germans found themselves preparing for the invasion of the European continent that was expected within months along the coast of France. In other words, the Nazis were even less able now than before to devote resources to development of an atomic bomb. Following the commando raid at Vemork, the Nazi atomic weapons program would never recover.

Although Einstein and other scientists expressed fears in 1939 that the Germans were well on the way to developing an atomic bomb, in reality neither the German nor the Japanese governments had kept pace with the American effort. The US government poured tremendous resources into the development of the atomic bomb, constructing huge facilities in Hanford and Oak Ridge as well as the laboratory at Los Alamos. With the world's top scientific minds working on development of the bomb at Los Alamos, by early 1945 it was clear the Allies would win the race against the Germans and the Japanese, and the end of the war was within sight.

Chapter 4

Fat Man and Little Boy

By February 1945 German forces were in retreat. Caught between the Allied advance to their west and the Soviet advance to their east, the Germans could not sustain a two-front war. By April Allied and Soviet troops were advancing on Berlin. Hitler committed suicide on April 30, and on May 8 the Nazi regime surrendered.

But the war in the Pacific raged on. Despite a string of defeats throughout 1944 and early 1945, the Japanese military refused to surrender. Starting in late 1944, Japanese pilots were assigned to suicidal kamikaze missions. With bombs implanted in the noses of their planes, it was the job of the kamikaze pilots to fly through enemy fire, crashing their planes into Allied warships. Throughout 1944 and 1945 more than twenty-five hundred Japanese pilots flew kamikaze missions. In English, *kamikaze* means "divine wind." The Japanese had given that name to the storms that sunk fleets of Mongol ships preparing to lay siege to Japan in the thirteenth century.

As American forces fought the Japanese army island to island, American casualties were high. By 1945 more than one hundred thousand Americans would be killed in the war against the Japanese. In the culture of the Japanese military, surrender was not an option. As American troops stormed Pacific islands, they would find Japanese soldiers hiding in caves. Invariably, the Japanese soldiers would refuse to emerge from the caves, forcing the Americans to shoot their way in. "Thousands of our Marines and soldiers died rooting Japanese from the foxholes and bunkers when they were perfectly aware that their situation was hopeless,"[31] recalled Charlton Ogburn Jr., a US intelligence officer during the war.

Facing this degree of resolve, Allied military leaders knew the Japanese would never surrender until their military was decisively vanquished. Thus, in 1944 military leaders started planning Operation Downfall—the invasion of Japan. Secretary of War Henry Stimson lamented, "It is a grim fact that there is not an easy, bloodless way to victory."[32]

One Million Allied Casualties

Unlike the June 1944 invasion of Europe, in which Allied troops could rely on the sympathies and help from the occupied peoples of France and other European countries, no such help would be available on the ground in Japan. In addition to the prospect of facing some 5 million Japanese soldiers defending their homeland, the Japanese government was believed to be arming and training civilians to fight against the Allied invaders.

Military planners expected an amphibious invasion of Japan would require some 2.5 million Allied soldiers, sailors, and airmen, and that the fighting on the ground could extend into 1946. To accomplish the invasion, the Allies planned to withdraw troops from Europe following the defeat of Germany and ship them to the Pacific to bolster the forces already on duty there. Military planners estimated Allied casualties as high as 1 million. To President Harry Truman, the loss of so many lives of Americans and their allies was unthinkable.

Truman ascended to the presidency after the death of Roosevelt on April 12, 1945. Truman had seen combat for himself: He had served in the US Army during World War I, fighting against German soldiers. He knew firsthand the brutality of ground combat and wanted to avoid the unnecessary loss of American lives at all costs. As the new president pondered the use of the atomic bomb to end the war, he wrote to his wife, Bess, "I'll say that we'll end the war a year sooner now, and think of the kids who won't be killed! That's the important thing."[33]

Key Conclusions

On May 9, Truman held the first of several meetings with diplomatic and military advisers to discuss the possibility of ending the war by

A Japanese fighter plane on a kamikaze mission is shot down by antiaircraft guns on a US aircraft carrier in January 1945. In the culture of the Japanese military, surrender was not an option.

dropping atomic bombs on Japanese cities. Over the next few weeks Truman and his aides summoned scientists and other officials from the Manhattan Project for briefings on the status of their research. On June 1, Truman and his aides met one final time and came to three key conclusions:

- Atomic bombs should be used against Japan as soon as possible.
- The primary targets should be cities where armaments industries are concentrated; moreover, it is understood civilian casualties would be high.

- To maximize the psychological impact on the Japanese people and their leaders, and to convince them of the futility of carrying on the war, the bombs should be used without warning.

The third conclusion—that the bombs should be dropped without warning—had been the subject of considerable debate among Truman and his advisers. John J. McCloy, the assistant secretary of war, argued for informing the Japanese that the United States possessed atomic weapons and the bombs were capable of wiping out entire cities. "I said I would tell them [the Japanese] we have the bomb and I would tell them what kind of weapon it is," said McCloy. "And then I would tell them the surrender terms."[34]

Others suggested that a demonstration be staged and that Japanese leaders be summoned to witness it. Finally, Truman and his top aides decided that, given the resolve of the Japanese military, to produce an unconditional Japanese surrender the United States had no choice but to demonstrate the capability of the bomb by actually using it. Stimson later stated, "I felt that to extract a genuine surrender from the Emperor and his military advisers, there must be administered a tremendous shock which would carry convincing proof of our power to destroy the Empire."[35]

Two Designs

During the meetings with Manhattan Project scientists, it became clear to Truman and his aides that the scientists wanted the opportunity to test the bomb before deploying the weapon under battlefield conditions. In the months leading up to the meetings with Truman and his aides, the Manhattan Project scientists had been working on two bomb designs—one that used U-235, the other plutonium.

The U-235 bomb was originally known as Thin Man, a nickname to honor the gaunt Roosevelt. (Soon, the engineers and scientists dubbed the bomb "Little Boy," and that is the name forever associated with the bomb.) The slender bomb measured 10 feet (3 m) in length and 2 feet (0.7 m) in diameter, but it weighed nearly 9,000 pounds (4,082 kg). Inside the bomb, engineers designed a gun in which a small mass of

Why Was Nagasaki Bombed?

The atomic bomb was dropped on Hiroshima without warning to deliver a shock to the Japanese people, convincing them of the futility of continuing the war. Since sixty-eight thousand people initially were killed in the bombing of Hiroshima, why was it necessary to carry out a second bombing?

The second bombing was, in fact, authorized even before the *Enola Gay* left Tinian on the morning of August 6, 1945. Moreover, General Groves was ordered to prepare bombs for subsequent attacks on Japanese cities. President Truman and others believed it might take several bombings to convince the Japanese to give up the fight.

After the August 6 bombing the Japanese were slow to respond to what had occurred at Hiroshima. The damage was so severe that all communications with the city were down, and many officials were not sure what had occurred. Even among the Japanese leaders who knew of the devastation, many hard-liners still opposed surrender.

A day before the Nagasaki bombing, the Japanese botched a diplomatic overture to end the war: They appealed to the Soviets to broker a peace. At the time the Soviets had not entered the war against the Japanese. However, by then Soviet leader Joseph Stalin had learned of the Hiroshima bombing and told the Japanese his country now considered itself at war with Japan. Soviet troops crossed over into China a few hours later and attacked Japanese positions; on August 9, the bombing of Nagasaki was carried out.

U-235 would be fired at a similar mass of U-235; the impact of the two masses of uranium would spark the chain reaction.

The second bomb design was known as Fat Man, a nickname in

honor of British prime minister Winston Churchill—a politician of considerable girth. Fat Man weighed nearly 10,000 pounds (4,536 kg). Its length was about 11 feet (3.5 m), and it was 5 feet (1.5 m) in diameter—more than twice the diameter of Little Boy. Fat Man used plutonium, with the chain reaction ignited in a variation of the implosion technique employed in the atomic cannons. Inside the bomb, the plutonium was encased in a device that resembled a soccer ball. Surrounding the ball were sixty-four conventional explosives. When the explosives were detonated, the shock waves slammed into the plutonium, compressing the mass. The increase in density would then spark a chain reaction within the mass of plutonium.

The Manhattan Project scientists had less confidence in the Fat Man design than in Little Boy, and so it was decided the test would involve the detonation of the plutonium bomb. The site selected for the test was a patch of desert in New Mexico about 200 miles (322 km) south of Los Alamos. Located 47 miles (76 km) from the town of Alamogordo, the test site was on military-owned property where the armed forces tested ordnance.

Code Name: Trinity

Oppenheimer conceived the code name for the test: Trinity. Oppenheimer never explained the reason behind the name, but historians have speculated that Oppenheimer believed the test reflected the biblical explanation for the three phases, or trinity, of existence on earth: life, death, and resurrection. In other words, the bomb would cause suffering and death, but it would also preserve lives by ending the war and give birth to a new world free of totalitarianism.

Plans had actually been under way to make the test since late 1944. Because of the heavy equipment that had to be transported to the site, roads had to be built. Scientists and engineers would have to spend months in preparation for the test, so housing had to be built in the desert. Water had to be trucked in. It was the lack of these amenities that made the site so perfect for the test—its remote location and desolation would help enhance security.

The bombs that would be dropped on Japan were given the names Fat Man and Little Boy. Bomb cases for both are displayed at a museum in Los Alamos, New Mexico.

To perform the test, Fat Man would be hoisted to the top of a 100-foot (30 m) tower and suspended in the air to mimic the conditions under which it would be detonated as it fell from an airplane. To enable the scientists to observe the test, engineers erected bunkers in the desert soil. The first bunker was located 5,000 feet (1,524 m) from the test site, and the second was built 10,000 feet (3,048 m) from the site. Most of the staff planned to watch the test from an observation point located even farther away—10 miles (16 km) from the tower.

Tearing Through the Sky

The test was originally scheduled for July 17, 1945, but Truman asked the scientists to stage the test a day earlier. The reason: Truman was scheduled to meet with Churchill and Soviet leader Joseph Stalin on July 17 in Potsdam, Germany, to discuss the administration of postwar Europe. Clearly, Truman felt his bargaining position would be enhanced if he was able to attend the meeting as a world leader armed with an atomic weapon. And so Groves agreed to stage the test on July 16.

On July 14, a Saturday, the plutonium was inserted into the bomb. Fat Man was then hoisted into place at the top of the tower. The scientists spent Sunday fretting over the weather as a storm had blown through that day. If the storm persisted, the test would be canceled out of fear that heavy winds would carry dangerous radiation miles away from the test site, endangering populated areas. Later Sunday the weather improved, and orders were given to explode the bomb at 5:30 a.m. on Monday.

In the darkness of that morning, a party of scientists armed the detonation device in the bomb and then hastened to their vehicles to escape from the test site. Making it to the bunkers, the scientists and other observers were ordered to lie on their stomachs with their feet facing the blast. Everyone was told not to look at the initial flash; it could be so bright that it could cause blindness. Even after the initial blast, observers were told to use welder's glass to observe the test site.

At 5:10 a.m., the countdown began. With forty-five seconds to detonation, the final switch was thrown, putting the firing mechanism on automatic—there was no stopping it now. At the recorded time of 5:29:45 a.m., the bomb tore through the predawn New Mexico sky. Recalled physicist Otto Frisch, who witnessed the explosion,

> The sand hills at the very edge of the desert were shimmering in very bright light, almost colourless and shapeless. This light did not seem to change for a couple of seconds and then began to dim. I turned round, but that object on the horizon which looked like a small sun was still too bright to look at. I kept blinking and trying to take looks, and after another ten seconds or so it had grown and dimmed into something more like a huge oil fire. . . .

The Flawed Mission

The bombing of Hiroshima was carried out flawlessly, but that was not the case with the second atomic bomb mission, which occurred on August 9, 1945. In fact, the original target for the *Bockscar*—the B-29 that dropped the atomic bomb on Nagasaki—was the city of Kokura, where a huge arsenal was located. (*Bockscar* was named after its original pilot, Frederick Bock; however, on the bombing run the plane was flown by Captain Charles W. Sweeney. Bock flew an observation plane on the mission.)

As Sweeney approached Kokura, the plane encountered flak—antiaircraft shots fired from the ground. "We had some flak bursts and things were getting a little hairy, so . . . Sweeney decided to make a run down to Nagasaki, as there was no sense dragging the bomb home or dropping it in the ocean," recalled a crew member.

Nagasaki is about 100 miles (161 km) west of Kokura. The *Bockscar* released the bomb over the city at 11:02 a.m. By then the plane was running short of fuel due to a malfunctioning fuel pump. The *Bockscar* could not make it back to its base at Tinian, about 1,600 miles (2,575 km) from Japan; instead, it flew to the island of Okinawa, located just 400 miles (644 km) from Japan. By the time the *Bockscar* landed at Okinawa, its fuel tanks were virtually empty; the plane lacked the fuel to taxi off the runway.

Quoted in Gerard J. DeGroot, *The Bomb: A Life*. Cambridge, MA: Harvard University Press, 2004, p. 99.

It was an awesome spectacle. . . . And all in complete silence; the bang came minutes later, quite loud enough though I had plugged my ears, and followed by a long rumble of heavy traffic far away. I can still hear it.[36]

Others who witnessed the blast felt a deep sense of accomplishment. After toiling for years on the Manhattan Project, the gadget actually worked. Some of the scientists who witnessed the Trinity test jumped to their feet and cheered. As for Oppenheimer, he found himself recalling a passage from the Bhagavad Gita, an ancient text that tells the story of the Hindu religion: "I am become Death, the destroyer of worlds."[37]

The Targets

As the Manhattan Project scientists prepared and then executed the Trinity test, military leaders were examining possible targets for the bomb. A Target Committee, headed by Groves, started meeting April 27, 1945. The committee, composed of military officers, scientists, and explosives experts, established criteria for the target: The city had to be densely populated but also have strategic value as a center for the Japanese armaments industry. Also, to protect Allied prisoners of war (POWs), the Target Committee did not want to bomb a city near where a POW camp was located.

Moreover, since 1944 the Allies had been flying conventional bombing missions over Japan and had already inflicted significant damage on several major cities, including Tokyo. To maximize the psychological impact of the atomic bomb, the Target Committee considered only cities that had thus far escaped conventional Allied bombing. Eventually five cities made the list: Hiroshima, Kokura, Nigata, Kyoto, and Nagasaki. When Stimson saw the list, he exercised his authority and deleted Kyoto as a target. Prior to the war he had visited Kyoto—the location of ancient Japanese shrines—and knew that if the atomic bomb destroyed the shrines the Japanese would never forgive the Americans, meaning that postwar relations between the two countries would remain cold.

Hiroshima was designated as the primary target. Japan's fourth-largest city was an industrial center of some three hundred thousand residents. It also met the criteria of having escaped bombardment over the course of the war. Finally, no POW camps were known to be located nearby.

The 509th Composite Group

The job of dropping the bomb fell to the US Army's 509th Composite Group, a bomber force. In the months prior to the Trinity test, the group's B-29 bombers had been specially fitted to accommodate the bombs at a military airbase in Wendover, Utah. As with most Manhattan Project sites, Wendover Field was selected for its seclusion; it was located in the Utah desert, about 125 miles (201 km) west of Salt Lake City. The bomber crews started training at Wendover in September 1944. The crews were veterans of bombing campaigns in Europe, and they found the conditions under which they trained in Utah much different. In Europe they flew night missions with little visibility as flak exploded around them. Now they were flying through crystal-clear desert skies. If the crew members did wonder what they were training to do, they could not expect answers: Under orders from Groves, the bomber crews were not briefed on the purpose of the training.

On June 10, 1945, the planes of the 509th Composite Group flew to Tinian, a Pacific Ocean island about 1,600 miles (2,575 km) from Japan, where the crew training continued. During these practice runs over open ocean, the planes dropped dummy mock-ups of Fat Man and Little Boy. Meanwhile, the pilots and other crew members were still kept ignorant of the true nature of the payloads they were going to be asked to carry.

By late July the group's senior officers decided no additional training was needed—the crews were prepared to carry out the mission. The bombing of Hiroshima was scheduled for August 1, but a typhoon blew through the Pacific, delaying the mission. It was only on August 4 that the commander of the bomber group, Colonel Paul Tibbets, confided to the crew members that they had been selected to drop the atomic bomb on Hiroshima.

The Flight of the *Enola Gay*

The plan called for seven bombers to make the flight: Three planes would fly ahead as scouts; two would accompany the bombing plane to photograph the mission; one would carry out the bombing; and the seventh would also carry an atomic weapon, acting as a backup. By August 5, the weather improved and the order was given to commence the flight early the next morning.

Tibbets elected to fly the plane carrying the Little Boy bomb. (Across the bomb someone had scrawled the message, "Greetings to the Emperor.") On the day before the flight, Tibbets had the name of his mother, Enola Gay, stenciled onto the plane's nose. At 2:27 a.m. on August 6, the *Enola Gay* took off from Tinian.

On the ground in Japan, the scout planes were spotted before 8 a.m. Air raid sirens sounded, a somewhat routine occurrence in a country that had been at war for four years. When other Japanese cities had been attacked by conventional bombers, dozens of enemy planes had filled the sky. But with just three planes visible overhead, the Japanese did not believe a major bombing run was under way. To many citizens of Hiroshima, it hardly seemed worth the trouble to head for the bomb shelters.

Just before 8 a.m. the *Enola Gay* approached Hiroshima. Bombardier Thomas Ferebee opened the bomb bay doors of the plane. At 8:14 a.m. Ferebee released the bomb. While falling 1,900 feet (580 m) over Hiroshima, the trigger mechanism in the bomb activated. The gun inside Little Boy fired, shooting a mass of U-235 and sparking the chain reaction. The actual time of the explosion was recorded at 8:16 a.m. What happened next was described by Robert Caron, the tail gunner aboard the *Enola Gay*:

> A column of smoke is rising fast. It has a fiery red core. A bubbling mass, purple grey in colour, with that red core. It's all turbulent. Fires are springing up everywhere, like flames shooting out of a huge bed of coals. . . .
>
> Here it comes, the mushroom shape. . . . It's like a mass of bubbling molasses. The mushroom is spreading out. It's maybe a mile or two wide and half a mile high. . . .
>
> The city must be below that. The flames and smoke are billowing out, whirling out into the foothills. The hills are disappearing under the smoke.[38]

About seven months after the United States dropped an atomic bomb on Hiroshima, an aerial view shows a bridge and a few skeletal parts of buildings but little else on the ground. The fireball that swept through the city caught residents completely off guard.

Another member of the *Enola Gay* crew also recorded his comments that morning. Making notes in his log book, copilot Robert Lewis wrote, "My God, what have we done?"[39]

Ground Zero

The fireball swept through the city, catching the residents completely off guard. A physician, Michihiko Hachiya, recalled that it had been a pleasant summer morning in the city, with the temperature hovering around 80°F (27°C). As he traveled to his job at a local hospital that morning, Hachiya recalled passing Japanese soldiers, stripped to their waists, performing calisthenics. Thousands of schoolgirls had been summoned to the city's center to help clear debris regarded as fire hazards in the event of an Allied bombing attack. One of the girls helping to clear the debris recalled the voice of her teacher telling the students that she could see a bomber approaching overhead. At that point, the girl said, "We felt a tremendous flash of lightning. In an instant we were blinded and everything was just a frenzy of delirium."[40]

Later, scientific analyses of ground zero—the center of Hiroshima—found that the temperature had reached 5,400°F (2,982°C). People, animals, insects—all living things—that were touched by the bomb were incinerated, destroyed in the flash. When inspectors entered the scene, they found ashes in the shapes of human beings on the streets. Most everything in the path of the flash, including buildings, bridges, and trees, was incinerated. Yoko Ota, a survivor, recalled that "there was a fearful silence which made one feel that all people and all trees and all vegetation were dead."[41]

As many as sixty-eight thousand people were killed that morning as the atomic bomb destroyed much of the city of Hiroshima. Another seventy thousand would die in the ensuing weeks and months from radiation poisoning. On August 9, another crew aboard the B-29 *Bockscar* dropped the Fat Man bomb on the city of Nagasaki, causing some thirty-eight thousand deaths immediately, with thirty-five thousand to follow in later weeks and months. On August 14, the Japanese agreed to an unconditional surrender.

Chapter 5

What Is the Legacy of the Making of the Atomic Bomb?

It was Roosevelt who first envisioned the power of the atomic bomb beyond its use as a weapon to vanquish the Germans and Japanese. Armed with such a devastating weapon, Roosevelt saw the United States emerging from World War II as the mightiest nation on the planet. The American president harbored no visions of international conquest; rather, Roosevelt saw the atomic bomb as a vehicle to help America spread democracy. Facing the devastating consequences of an atomic bomb, Roosevelt reasoned, no enemy would rise up against American principles. Therefore, Roosevelt believed, the atomic bomb would make conventional warfare obsolete. As historians Campbell Craig and Sergey Radchenko explain, "He believed that a United States in a position of preponderant power at the end of the war could impose these frameworks [of democracy] on a beaten world and, this time, genuinely make the Second World War a war to end all wars."[42]

Roosevelt died before the United States loosed its atomic weapons on Hiroshima and Nagasaki, so he never saw the bomb's devastating powers or its psychological impact on the world. Many of those who did soon echoed Roosevelt's beliefs, suggesting that conventional warfare—in which armies are summoned to face one another on the battlefield—would no longer be a part of life on earth.

Following the destruction of Hiroshima and Nagasaki, Secretary of War Henry Stimson said the bombings were "the only way to awaken the world to the necessity of abolishing war altogether. No technical demonstration . . . could take the place of the actual use with its horrible results."[43] And in the days following the destruction of Hiroshima and Nagasaki, Truman declared, "We thank God that it has come to us, instead of our enemies; and we pray that He may guide us to use it in His ways and for His purposes."[44]

Mutual Assured Destruction

When Stimson, Truman, and others made those predictions about the end of conventional warfare, they did not foresee the events of August 29, 1949. That was the day the Soviet Union conducted a successful test of its own atomic bomb. There were now two superpowers armed with atomic weapons, and they were rivals for influence throughout the world. It was the dawn of the Cold War—the post–World War II era in which the United States and the Soviet Union vied for dominance among the nations of the world. The Soviets, under the ruthless dictator Stalin and, later, similarly despotic leaders, sought to spread the principles of communism throughout Eastern Europe and eventually to the Western Hemisphere. In 1956, as he addressed a group of Western diplomats at a reception at the Polish embassy in Moscow, Soviet leader Nikita Khrushchev gave voice to the tensions of the era when he warned, "History is on our side. We will bury you."[45] Khrushchev made that off-the-cuff remark as a popular uprising was under way in Hungary, that threatened to topple the Soviet-backed Communist regime. Soon, the Soviets dispatched troops to restore order and put down the uprising.

And, as events would soon prove, the existence of atomic weapons would not make conventional warfare obsolete. Following World War II, the American military would be deployed to the Korean Peninsula and later Vietnam to counter Communist movements backed by the Soviet Union or its ally, China. With both sides armed with atomic weapons, now generally known as nuclear weapons, neither side dared use them. This policy was soon known as mutual assured destruction (MAD). In simple terms, the MAD policy ensured that if one side deployed nuclear weapons, the other side would unleash its own nuclear arsenal. By the 1960s the United States and the Soviet Union possessed so many atomic weapons that each side held the power to virtually wipe out human civilization.

Indeed, the Soviet test of 1949 sparked an arms race between the two superpowers as each side refined and developed even more devastating weapons. By the early 1960s the United States was known to have developed the Mark 39 atomic bomb, a weapon believed to have 260 times the destructive power of Little Boy. The arms race—and the possibility that human civilization could be wiped off the planet with the push of a button—came to dominate virtually all aspects of life in the 1950s and beyond. According to writer Bruce Watson, "Throughout the '50s, in fact, 'the bomb' was an unwanted guest at the postwar American dream party. While the economy boomed and the public sunbathed in self-assurance, rumbling headlines about atomic weapons pitted prosperity against panic in a Cold War of the American mind."[46]

In 1949 Einstein gave voice to the fears of atomic warfare. When an interviewer asked Einstein whether he thought World War III would be fought with atomic weapons, the great mathematician replied that he would not speculate about that, but if such a scenario were to unfold, he was quite certain World War IV would be fought with stones.

Duck and Cover

As Einstein's remarks illustrated, the atomic era was serious business. No incident exemplified the fear of an atomic arms race more than the revelation that during the 1940s two Americans, Julius and Ethel Rosenberg, headed a spy ring that had stolen scientific documents from the Los Alamos laboratory and supplied them to the Soviets, evidently helping the Soviets develop the atomic bomb. In 1951 the Rosenbergs were tried and convicted of espionage; they were executed two years later.

The Rosenberg case helped mark the birth of a great anti-Communist fervor in American society. This campaign was punctuated by the witch hunts and fear mongering of the 1950s by Wisconsin senator Joseph McCarthy and the House Un-American Activities Committee

Julius and Ethel Rosenberg leave federal court in 1950 after being indicted on charges of espionage. The case against the couple exemplified fears of a nuclear arms race.

(HUAC). Both waged campaigns that accused many innocent Americans of maintaining ties to Communist groups.

Fueling this campaign was a fear that Communist infiltration of American life and values would change America from a free society to one ruled by a totalitarian regime and marked by government ownership of industry and property. Yet the dominant fear of the era found Americans believing that if Communists gained a foothold in the American government and military, the nation's atomic secrets would be turned over to Moscow. American leaders believed that atomic science in the United State had progressed far in advance of what the Soviets had accomplished, and they did not want those secrets falling into Soviet hands. In 1950 McCarthy announced on the Senate floor that at least fifty key American atomic scientists maintained ties to Communist organizations. It was a false charge typical of the era; nevertheless, it earned headlines for the senator and helped stoke fears of nuclear war with the Soviets. Gordon Dean, the chair of the US Atomic Energy Commission, the civilian agency charged with overseeing atomic research, responded to McCarthy's charges: "It is deplorable that statements of the type made by Senator McCarthy tend to undermine confidence in the atomic energy program in defiance of the facts."[47]

Eventually even Oppenheimer—whose work on the Manhattan Project may have helped save the lives of 1 million American servicemen—found his loyalty questioned. Called before the HUAC, Oppenheimer admitted that as a young man he had sympathized with Communist movements—a revelation that resulted in a revocation of his security clearance in 1953. Lacking the clearance, Oppenheimer could no longer work on projects related to fission.

As the loyalty of scientists like Oppenheimer was questioned, Americans convinced themselves they had much to fear. During the 1950s many Americans dug up their backyards to build underground shelters, stocking them with canned food and bottled water in the belief they would provide refuge in the event Soviet planes suddenly appeared over American cities, raining Hiroshima-style bombs onto their neighborhoods. One company that installed shelters in Southern California issued pamphlets to homeowners advising them to expect widespread devastation when they emerged from their shelters after the bombs had dropped: "Things are probably going to look different when you get outside,"[48] the pamphlets cautioned. Meanwhile, in American schools students were taught the duck-and-cover technique, suggesting, quite emphatically, that in the event of a nuclear attack during the school day, they would have the best chance of surviving by hiding under their desks.

Who Was Bert the Turtle?

To help teach schoolchildren how to react during an atomic bomb attack, in 1950 the Office of Civil Defense—a federal agency charged with emergency preparedness—created a cartoon character named Bert the Turtle. Bert's job was to convince schoolchildren they could actually survive an atomic blast. Bert appeared in animated films as well as pamphlets and other printed literature, giving lessons to young people on how to duck and cover when the bombs start falling.

To protect themselves against the bright flash, intense heat, and flying debris of the atomic explosion, children were taught to duck (to look away from the blast) and find cover (by hiding under their desks). To illustrate the proper duck-and-cover technique, Bert was shown withdrawing his head into his shell to wait out the blast. According to one pamphlet distributed to schoolchildren in the 1950s,

> You have learned how to take care of yourself in many ways—to cross streets safely. And you know what to do in case of fire—but the atomic bomb is a new danger. It explodes with a flash brighter than any you've ever seen. . . . Things will be knocked down all over town, and, as in a big wind are blown through the air. So, like Bert, you DUCK to avoid the things flying through the air . . . and COVER to keep from getting cut or badly burned.

Quoted in Tod Olson, "In the Shadow of the Bomb," *Scholastic Update*, March 16, 1998, p. 25.

The Missile Crisis

By the early 1960s McCarthy had been thoroughly discredited; he had died in 1957, just a few years after having been disciplined by the Senate on charges of making unsubstantiated attacks against innocent Americans. But the passing of the 1950s would not mean an end to the fear of annihilation by atomic weapons. Indeed, in October 1962 nuclear war surfaced as a distinct reality when a US Air Force spy plane flying over Cuba detected the presence of Soviet missile silos on the island, just 90 miles (145 km) from the Florida coast. The Soviets, believing themselves endangered by the threat of attacks by nuclear-armed American missiles, enlisted their ally Fidel Castro to establish a nuclear weapons base in Cuba. The Soviets lagged behind the Americans in missile development. Therefore, they did not have the capability to launch strikes on American cities from bases thousands of miles away. The Soviets believed the missile base in Cuba would help keep them even with the Americans in the arms race.

For two weeks the United States and the Soviet Union teetered on the brink of nuclear war as President John F. Kennedy demanded removal of the missiles and the dismantling of the base. Finally, on October 28, 1962, Khrushchev backed down and ordered the weapons to be withdrawn.

Following the Cuban Missile Crisis, tensions between the United States and the Soviet Union remained high, particularly since the two superpowers would soon engage in a proxy war in Vietnam. (The Americans backed the anti-Communist regime in South Vietnam, eventually providing troops for the war, and in North Vietnam the Soviets provided arms and other aid to the Communist regime.) But at least when it came to nuclear arms, diplomatic channels remained open. Starting in 1963 the United States, the Soviet Union, and other countries agreed to a series of treaties that limited testing of atomic weapons, reduced the nuclear arms stockpile, and outlawed atomic weapons in space. Since the 1990s the nonproliferation treaties have been signed by many governments, including the government in Russia, which replaced the Communist regime following the collapse of the Soviet Union. Thus, even though communism has ceased to threaten world freedom, the bombs left over from the Cold War remain.

Japan Embraces Atomic Energy

As world governments took steps to ensure they would not wage nuclear war on one another, the one country where atomic bombs had dropped—Japan—has worked hard to remember the victims of Hiroshima and Nagasaki. In the years since the end of the war, Japanese society has dedicated itself to honoring the memories of the victims of the two atomic blasts. Victims are known as *hibakusha*, a word that translates literally to "explosion-affected people." Of the tens of thousands of victims of the bombings, the story of Sadako Sasaki has endured. The young girl's fate is well known in Japan, and her story serves as a reminder to all Japanese of the devastating and long-term effects of atomic weapons.

Sasaki was two years old when the bomb exploded over Hiroshima. She was blasted out of the window of her home. Her mother found her in the rubble; remarkably, the child survived.

A decade later Sasaki developed symptoms of leukemia, a cancer of the blood and bone marrow. Sasaki died just weeks before her thirteenth birthday. Before her death, however, a friend had visited her in the hospital and had given her an origami crane. After this, Sasaki had folded more cranes herself, and her friends had folded them as well. At her funeral, Sasaki was buried with one thousand paper cranes. In Japanese culture the gift of one thousand paper cranes is believed to bring luck. A statue of Sasaki holding a crane has been erected in Hiroshima; it is regarded as a memorial to all the *hibakusha*. Each year on the Buddhist holiday of Obon, visitors place origami cranes at the base of the statue.

Despite the shadow of devastation that has hung over Japanese society since 1945, the Japanese people have learned to embrace atomic energy. In the 1950s, as nuclear power plants were developed, the Japanese saw atomic energy as a way to power their cities and help them build a powerful economy. According to the trade group World Nuclear Association, fifty nuclear reactors operate in Japan, producing 30 percent of the country's energy. (In contrast, nuclear power plants provide 19 percent of America's energy.)

Some activists in Japan see the country's dedication to atomic energy as contradictory: How can Japan honor and remember the *hibakusha* but still embrace nuclear power? In 2011 this debate found new life when a tsunami struck northern Japan, disabling the Fukushima Daiichi nuclear plant. Radiation was released from the plant, causing the temporary evacuations of tens of thousands of people from the region. Moreover, Japan is believed to have narrowly escaped a catastrophe when workers contained a leak of fissionable material—a circumstance

Atomic Energy and Electricity

The process pioneered in 1942 by Enrico Fermi to control the fission reaction was found to be an effective means for using atomic power to produce electricity. In the 1950s scientists developed pressure water reactors, which could use atomic energy to heat water, converting it to steam and then using it to turn turbines to produce electricity. Facilities employing such reactors are able to provide power for entire cities.

In the Chicago Pile experiment, Fermi controlled the fission reaction by withdrawing rods made of cadmium. The rods absorbed neutrons; as the rods were withdrawn, the fission reactions commenced. Nuclear power plants operate under fundamentally the same principle. The fissionable material employed in nuclear power plants is usually the uranium isotope U-235—the same fissionable material used in Little Boy, the bomb dropped on Hiroshima. In today's plants, cadmium and boron are the materials most frequently used in the composition of control rods.

As a safety measure, nuclear plants use great quantities of water to cool the fissionable material. Familiar sights at all nuclear plants are the huge cooling towers that vent steam into the atmosphere after water is used to cool the reactor cores. The first plant that employed nuclear power to make electricity went into service in Arco, Idaho, in 1955. Today 12 percent of the world's energy is produced through nuclear power plants.

that could have caused an explosion. "Is it Japan's fate to repeatedly serve as a warning to the world about the dangers of radiation?" asks eighty-one-year-old Masahito Hirose, who was a junior high school student in Nagasaki in 1945. "I wish we had found the courage to speak out earlier against nuclear power."[49]

The campaign to shut down Japanese nuclear power plants is led by Nihon Hidankyo, a group that represents an estimated fifty thousand survivors of the Hiroshima and Nagasaki blasts nearly seven decades ago. With atomic energy so key to the Japanese economy, leaders of Nihon Hidankyo face stiff opposition to their goal. However, there is evidence that some political leaders have embraced the idea. Former prime minister Naoto Kan, who led the Japanese government during the Fukushima accident, says, "There is only one way to eliminate such accidents, which is to get rid of all nuclear plants."[50]

Nuclear Nations

The threat of nuclear devastation no longer emanates from the Cold War but rather through the likelihood that a rogue state will acquire atomic weapons. In 2003 President George W. Bush convinced Congress to authorize the invasion of Iraq. This was largely based on intelligence that led Bush and his advisers to believe that Iraqi dictator Saddam Hussein had attempted to obtain quantities of uranium mined in the African nation of Niger. The intelligence eventually proved faulty. Nevertheless, the fear that a ruthless dictator could develop an atomic weapon was found to justify launching a war.

Despite the efforts by America and other countries to abide by treaties and control the proliferation of nuclear arms, nine countries are known to possess atomic weapons. In addition to America and Russia, the other nuclear-armed states are Great Britain, France, India, Pakistan, Israel, China, and North Korea. Of those states, diplomats find a nuclear-armed North Korea most alarming because the country is ruled by a Communist dictatorship that has maintained unfriendly terms with the West for more than sixty years.

China, however, with its movement toward a market-based

Students offer paper cranes at the Children's Peace Monument in the Peace Memorial Park in Hiroshima in 2010. The monument was built in memory of Sadako Sasaki, who survived the bombing of Hiroshima but died a decade later from leukemia likely caused by exposure to radiation.

economy and an interest in promoting trade with the West, is believed to exert considerable influence over the North Koreans. Indeed, the Chinese provide 90 percent of the energy and 80 percent of the food consumed in North Korea and have used their economic aid to rein in the North Korean nuclear program. In 2013, after the North Koreans conducted a nuclear test, the Chinese government claimed to have admonished the North Koreans against staging further tests. Soon after the North Korean test, Chinese foreign minister Wang Yi said his government "would not allow troublemaking at the doorsteps of China."[51]

A Dark Shadow

Other states have raised similar concerns. Following India's development of an atomic weapon in 1974, its neighbor and longtime enemy, Pakistan, felt compelled to develop its own weapon; in 1998 Pakistan successfully staged its first nuclear test. Now, two of the world's most hostile neighbors, India and Pakistan, possess the means to obliterate each other. And the fact that Islamic extremists have reportedly infiltrated the Pakistani government is unsettling to US officials, who have long claimed that Pakistan is a haven for terrorists.

Moreover, for years the Iranians have pursued the enrichment of uranium. As longtime enemies of the United States and known agitators in the Middle East, the notion of an Iranian atomic weapon is unacceptable to America and its allies. Iranian officials have claimed that the enrichment program is limited to the development of fuel for nuclear power plants, but Western diplomats and intelligence agencies suspect the Iranians have initiated a weapons program. The United States and dozens of other countries responded by imposing harsh economic measures on Iran, refusing to trade with the Middle East nation. These economic sanctions have meant that Iran, one of the most oil-rich countries on earth, found it nearly impossible to obtain consumer goods. With the Iranian middle class suffering, in 2013 the Iranian government sent diplomatic signals to the West indicating that it was ready to end its nuclear-enrichment program in exchange for an ease to the crippling economic sanctions. In late 2013 Western diplomats led by US secretary of state John Kerry announced an agreement with the Iranians in which the country promised to curtail its uranium-enrichment program.

The decision by the Iranians to curtail their weapons development program is an example of how an international dispute was settled at the bargaining table. That was always the dream of Leo Szilard, who dedicated his life to fission research, always hoping it would never be necessary to use the atomic bomb. He believed that once the world became aware of the enormous destructive power of the bomb, nations would, out of fear it would be used, learn to settle their disputes at the bargaining table rather than on the battlefield. Clearly, that dream has seldom been realized. Nor was the dream of Roosevelt realized—that once the world saw the destructive power of the bomb, conventional warfare would become obsolete. Neither Szilard nor Roosevelt considered what would happen if rival countries obtained atomic weapons, therefore raising the possibility of widespread nuclear warfare. But now nine nations possess nuclear weapons, and some of them—notably India and Pakistan—harbor long-standing grievances toward each other. Meanwhile, another nuclear power, North Korea, is headed by a despotic and unpredictable regime. Nearly seven decades after Hiroshima and Nagasaki were destroyed by atomic weapons, the destructive power of the fission reaction continues to cast a dark shadow over life on earth.

Source Notes

Introduction: The Defining Characteristics of the Making of the Atomic Bomb

1. H.G. Wells, *The World Set Free*. Fairbanks, AK: Project Gutenberg, 2006, e-book.
2. Hildegarde Hawthorne, "*The World Set Free*," *New York Times*, March 29, 1914, p. BR-141.
3. Anne Rooney, *The History of Physics*. New York: Rosen, 2013, p. 132.
4. Quoted in Michael Bess, "Leo Szilard: Scientist, Activist, Visionary," *Bulletin of the Atomic Scientists*, December 1985, p. 11.
5. Gerard J. DeGroot, *The Bomb: A Life*. Cambridge, MA: Harvard University Press, 2004, p. 33.

Chapter One: What Conditions Led to the Making of the Atomic Bomb?

6. Quoted in P.D. Smith, *Doomsday Men: The Real Dr. Strangelove and the Dream of the Superweapon*. New York: St. Martin's, 2007, p. 145.
7. Quoted in Richard Rhodes, *The Making of the Atomic Bomb*. New York: Simon & Schuster, 2012, p. 164.
8. Stephen M. Younger, *The Bomb: A New History*. New York: HarperCollins, 2009, pp. 14–15.
9. Quoted in DeGroot, *The Bomb*, p. 13.
10. Quoted in DeGroot, *The Bomb*, p. 17.
11. Quoted in Rhodes, *The Making of the Atomic Bomb*, p. 305.
12. Quoted in *American Experience: Truman,* "Letter from Albert Einstein to FDR, 8/2/39," 1997. www.pbs.org.
13. Quoted in Andrew J. Rotter, *Hiroshima: The World's Bomb*. Oxford, UK: Oxford University Press, 2008, p. 85.

Chapter Two: The Chicago Pile

14. Quoted in Robert LaRue, "Berkeley Summer: Building the Bomb," *World War II*, May 2000, p. 34.
15. Quoted in William J. Broad, "Why They Called It the Manhattan Project," *New York Times*, October 30, 2007. www.nytimes.com.
16. Quoted in Rhodes, *The Making of the Atomic Bomb*, pp. 448–49.
17. Kai Bird and Martin J. Sherwin, "Building the Bomb," *Smithsonian*, August 2005, p. 88.
18. Quoted in Bird and Sherwin, "Building the Bomb," p. 88.
19. Enrico Fermi, "The Chicago Pile-1: The First Chain Reaction," in *The Manhattan Project: The Birth of the Atomic Bomb in the Words of Its Creators, Eyewitnesses, and Historians,* ed. Cynthia C. Kelly. New York: Black Dog & Leventhal, 2007, p. 82.
20. Quoted in Rhodes, *The Making of the Atomic Bomb*, p. 440.
21. DeGroot, *The Bomb*, p. 49.

Chapter Three: Site Y

22. DeGroot, *The Bomb*, p. 39.
23. Quoted in DeGroot, *The Bomb,* p. 39.
24. Quoted in Kelly, ed., *The Manhattan Project*, p. 168.
25. Quoted in Rhodes, *The Making of the Atomic Bomb*, p. 451.
26. Quoted in DeGroot, *The Bomb,* p. 41.
27. Paul Olum, "Hiroshima: Memoir of a Bomb Maker," George Mason University History News Network, 2013. http://hnn.us.
28. Quoted in Kristie Macrakis, *Surviving the Swastika: Scientific Research in Nazi Germany.* New York: Oxford University Press, 1993, p. 52.
29. Quoted in Rhodes, *The Making of the Atomic Bomb*, p. 456.
30. Quoted in Rhodes, *The Making of the Atomic Bomb*, p. 457.

Chapter Four: Fat Man and Little Boy

31. Quoted in David McCullough, *Truman.* New York: Simon & Schuster, 1992, p. 438.
32. Quoted in D.M. Giangreco, *Hell to Pay: Operation Downfall and the Invasion of Japan, 1945–1947.* Annapolis: Naval Institute Press, 2009, p. xii.
33. Quoted in McCullough, *Truman,* p. 440.

34. Quoted in McCullough, *Truman,* p. 401.
35. Quoted in McCullough, *Truman*, p. 394.
36. Quoted in DeGroot, *The Bomb,* p. 61.
37. Quoted in Daniel J. Lenihan, "Ground Zero Revisited," *Natural History*, July 1995, p. 42.
38. Quoted in DeGroot, *The Bomb,* p. 85.
39. Quoted in DeGroot, *The Bomb,* p. 85.
40. Quoted in Rhodes, *The Making of the Atomic Bomb*, p. 714.
41. Quoted in Rhodes, *The Making of the Atomic Bomb*, p. 715.

Chapter Five: What Is the Legacy of the Making of the Atomic Bomb?

42. Campbell Craig and Sergey Radchenko, *The Atomic Bomb and the Origins of the Cold War.* New Haven, CT: Yale University Press, 2008, p. 4.
43. Quoted in H. Bruce Franklin, "Fatal Fiction: A Weapon to End All Wars," in *The Nightmare Considered: Critical Essays on Nuclear War Literature,* ed. Nancy Anisfield. Bowling Green, OH: Popular, 1991, p. 11.
44. Quoted in Franklin, "Fatal Fiction," p. 12.
45. Quoted in Alfred Lubrano, "Pioneering Year: Youth Culture . . . Civil Rights . . . the Suburbs . . . Women's Rights," *Philadelphia Inquirer*, August 4, 2006. http://articles.philly.com.
46. Bruce Watson, "We Couldn't Run, So We Hoped We Could Hide," *Smithsonian*, April 1994, p. 46.
47. Quoted in *Bulletin of the Atomic Scientists*, "McCarthy's New Accusations," November 1950, p. 352.
48. Quoted in Watson, "We Couldn't Run, So We Hoped We Could Hide," p. 46.
49. Quoted in Martin Fackler, "Atomic Bomb Survivors Join Nuclear Opposition," *New York Times*, August 7, 2011, p. A-11.
50. Quoted in David Biello, "The Nuclear Odyssey of Naoto Kan, Japan's Prime Minister During Fukushima," *Scientific American*, October 16, 2013. www.scientificamerican.com.
51. Quoted in Antoine Bondaz, "A New Direction for China's North Korea Policy," Carnegie-Tsinghua Center for Global Policy, August 27, 2013. http://m.ceip.org.

Important People in the Making of the Atomic Bomb

Vannevar Bush: Appointed by President Franklin D. Roosevelt to head the National Defense Research Committee (later the US Office of Scientific Research and Development), Bush was charged with assessing civilian scientific programs for their use by the military. Bush saw the potential of fission research and urged Roosevelt to make the Manhattan Project a priority—eventually Congress would provide $20 billion in funding for fission research.

James Chadwick: A British scientist, Chadwick confirmed the existence of a neutral particle in the atom known as the neutron. Although neutrons do not carry electrical charges, through the process of fission neutrons can be made to leave their host atoms and form new nuclei. Chadwick's experiments showed how the fission process would create a transfer of energy, a vital step in a chain reaction that would result in an atomic blast.

Marie Curie: A Polish-born French physicist, Curie determined that many elements, including uranium, emit particles in a phenomenon known as radioactivity. She provided much of the early research into uranium, measuring the energy dissipated by the element. Curie died in 1934 at the age of sixty-six, a victim of aplastic anemia—loss of blood cells in her bone marrow. Curie had been exposed to radioactivity throughout her research; her death showed that atomic weapons could have devastating effects on humans even if they survive the explosion.

Albert Einstein: In 1905 Einstein, a German-born mathematician, published the equation $E=mc^2$, establishing the mathematical principle on which fission could be produced. Thirty-four years later Einstein authored the letter that convinced President Roosevelt to establish a government-financed project to build an atomic bomb.

Enrico Fermi: An Italian-born physicist, Fermi won the Nobel Prize for showing how isotopes could be created during fission. After fleeing the Fascist regime of Benito Mussolini, Fermi worked on the Manhattan

Project. He headed the experiment to control a fission reaction and later helped solve the problem of critical mass—the amount of fissionable material it would take to spark a chain reaction in a bomb.

Leslie Groves: A no-nonsense general, Groves served in the US Army Corps of Engineers, the construction unit of the armed service. Prior to taking over the Manhattan Project, Groves had headed construction of the Pentagon in Washington, DC. Groves was obsessed with secrecy and decreed that only a handful of the Manhattan Project's top scientists should know the true purpose of their work. Groves also served on the panel that selected Hiroshima and Nagasaki as target cities for the bomb.

Otto Hahn and Fritz Strassmann: In 1938 German chemists Hahn and Strassmann bombarded uranium atoms with neutrons, creating a fission reaction in the laboratory and confirming that energy is released during an atomic chain reaction. Since their work was performed under Germany's Nazi regime, their achievement sent warning signals to scientists in America; they realized that in the hands of the Nazis, Hahn and Strassmann's work could be pursued for malevolent purposes.

Knut Haukelid: A Norwegian commando, Haukelid led a team that helped destroy the Nazi atomic weapons program. In 1943 commandos led by Haukelid successfully detonated explosives at a Nazi heavy water plant in Vemork, Norway. A year later Haukelid destroyed the last of the Nazi heavy water supply by sinking a ferry crossing Lake Tinnsjå in Norway. After the war Kurt Diebner, head of the German atomic weapons program, attributed the failure of the program to Haukelid's sabotage.

Lise Meitner: Meitner, an Austrian-born physicist, worked closely with Hahn and Strassmann to create a fission reaction in the laboratory, but Meitner, born Jewish, had to flee Germany before Hahn and Strassmann were able to prompt the chain reaction. Meitner did urge her colleagues to use uranium in the experiment, proving the element is highly volatile. After taking refuge in Sweden, Meitner refused an invitation to work on the Manhattan Project, declaring she wanted no role in creating a bomb.

Yoshino Nishina: A Japanese physicist, Nishina headed his country's atomic weapons program but was hampered by a lack of enthusiasm by his government in pursuing fission research. Only after Japan started suffering military defeats in 1943 did the Japanese government devote resources to fission research; by then the Japanese were well behind the American program and never managed to pursue effective fission research.

J. Robert Oppenheimer: Physicist Oppenheimer was asked by Groves to serve as civilian director of the Manhattan Project; under Oppenheimer the talents of hundreds of scientists were coordinated into the singular goal of creating an atomic weapon. Oppenheimer also convinced Groves to establish the project's central laboratory in Los Alamos, New Mexico. After the war Oppenheimer admitted to harboring sympathies for Communists and was stripped of his security clearance.

Franklin D. Roosevelt: US president Roosevelt took office in 1933 and served until his death in 1945, shortly before the end of World War II. Roosevelt created the Advisory Committee on Uranium, an organization that would eventually become the Manhattan Project. Roosevelt had hoped the atomic bomb would make conventional warfare obsolete and help America spread democracy. He died before the first atomic bomb was deployed.

Leo Szilard: Inspired by the science-fiction novel *The World Set Free*, Szilard, a Hungarian-born physicist, dedicated his life to fission research. In 1933 he conceived the process of how chain reactions could be sparked by the release of neutrons from atomic nuclei. Six years later he convinced Einstein to write to Roosevelt, advising the president of the dangers of the Nazi atomic weapons program.

Paul Tibbets: The commander of the US Army's 509th Composite Group, Tibbets elected to fly the plane that dropped the atomic bomb on the city of Hiroshima, Japan. Tibbets named the B-29 bomber the *Enola Gay* after his mother.

Harry Truman: As vice president under Roosevelt, Truman ascended to the presidency following Roosevelt's death on April 12, 1945, and almost immediately found himself confronted with the decision to use the atomic bomb on Japanese cities. Faced with the prospect of a long siege on the Japanese mainland, which could cost the lives of nearly 1 million Allied servicemen, Truman elected to use the bomb and to do so without warning.

For Further Research

Books

Paul Bracken, *The Second Nuclear Age: Strategy, Danger, and the New Power Politics.* New York: Times, 2012.

Craig Collie, *Nagasaki: The Massacre of the Innocent and Unknowing.* Sydney: Allen & Unwin, 2012.

Feroz Khan, *Eating Grass: The Making of the Pakistani Bomb.* Stanford, CA: Stanford University Press, 2012.

William Lanouette, *Genius in the Shadows: A Biography of Leo Szilard, the Man Behind the Bomb.* New York: Skyhorse, 2013.

Wilson D. Miscamble, *The Most Controversial Decision: Truman, the Atomic Bombs, and the Defeat of Japan.* New York: Cambridge University Press, 2011.

Ray Monk, *Robert Oppenheimer: His Life and Mind.* New York: Random House, 2013.

Richard Rhodes, *The Making of the Atomic Bomb.* New York: Simon & Schuster, 2012.

Spencer R. Weart, *The Rise of Nuclear Fear.* Cambridge, MA: Harvard University Press, 2012.

Websites

American Experience: The Trials of J. Robert Oppenheimer (www.pbs.org/wgbh/americanexperience/films/oppenheimer). This is a companion website to the 2009 film *The Trials of J. Robert Oppenheimer*, which was featured as part of the PBS series *American Experience*. Visitors can find a transcript of the film, which explores the life and work of Oppenheimer, as well as a photo gallery of images from the Manhattan Project and an overview of nuclear arms proliferation since the 1940s.

American Experience: Truman (www.pbs.org/wgbh/americanexperience/features/primary-resources/truman-ein39). This website accompanies the 1997 film *Truman*, featured on the PBS series *American Experience*. Visitors can find the text of the 1939 letter written by Einstein to Roosevelt in which he urges Roosevelt to organize an American fission research program. A video chronicling Truman's decision to use the bomb on Japan is also available.

Atomic Archive (www.atomicarchive.com). Sponsored by the National Science Foundation, this website provides many resources on the Manhattan Project. Visitors can follow links that provide an explanation of fission; a chronology of important events in the history of atomic physics; videos and photographs, including images of Fat Man and Little Boy; and biographies of Groves, Oppenheimer, and other key figures in atomic research.

Boeing B-29 Superfortress *Enola Gay* (http://airandspace.si.edu/collections/artifact.cfm?id=a19500100000). Maintained by the Smithsonian National Air and Space Museum, this webpage chronicles the mission of the *Enola Gay*, which is on display at the museum's Steven F. Udvar-Hazy Center in Chantilly, Virginia. Visitors will find a history of the B-29 bomber and learn how the planes assigned to the US Army's 509th Composite Group were modified to carry atomic bombs.

Cuban Missile Crisis (www.jfklibrary.org/JFK/JFK-in-History/Cuban-Missile-Crisis.aspx). This webpage, maintained by the John F. Kennedy Presidential Library and Museum, provides an overview of the October 1962 Cuban Missile Crisis, the event in which the United States and the Soviet Union came dangerously close to nuclear war. Visitors will find links for radio and television coverage of the crisis as well as an interactive timeline that provides an overview of the thirteen key days during the crisis.

Einstein's Big Idea (www.pbs.org/wgbh/nova/physics/einstein-big-idea.html). This webpage, which is a companion to the 2005 *Nova* episode by the same name, includes an explanation of the science behind Einstein's equation of $E=mc^2$ that suggested the existence of atomic fission. The webpage also includes a transcript of the broadcast, which provides an overview of the equation and Einstein's research as well as audio files of ten physicists explaining the equation.

How the First Chain Reaction Changed Science (www.uchicago.edu/features/how_the_first_chain_reaction_changed_science). Sponsored by the University of Chicago, this webpage provides a history of the experiment on December 2, 1942, in which Manhattan Project scientists were first able to control the fission reaction. In addition to the story of the experiment, visitors will find an explanation of the science of fission as well as a slide show of images and the video *How the Atomic Age Began at UChicago*.

Los Alamos National Laboratory (www.lanl.gov). More than seven decades after it was established during the Manhattan Project, the Los Alamos National Laboratory continues to serve as an important center of science, exploring research into atomic physics. By following the link for "History" on the laboratory's website, visitors can find an overview of the Manhattan Project as well as images from the era.

Index

Note: Boldface page numbers indicate illustrations.

Picture Credits

Cover: US National Archives and Records Administration/Science Photo Library

Maury Aaseng: 44

© Bettmann/Corbis: 35, 57, 67, 72

© Corbis: 50

© DK Limited/Corbis: 21, 38

© Wolfgang Kaehler/Corbis: 61

Kyodo/Newscom: 79

© Roger Ressmeyer/Corbis: 13

Science Source: 46

© The Print Collector/Corbis: 26

Thinkstock Images: 8, 9

Albert Einstein (1879–1955) c. 1922 (b/w photo), French Photographer, (20th century)/Private Collection/Archives Charmet/ The Bridgeman Art Library: 16

USS West Virginia and USS Tennessee on fire during the Japanese attack on Pearl Harbor, 7th December, 1941 (photo), American Photographer, (20th century)/ Private Collection/Peter Newark Military Pictures/The Bridgeman Art Library: 29

About the Author

Hal Marcovitz is a former newspaper reporter and columnist. He is the author of more than 150 books for young readers. His other titles in the Understanding World History series include *Ancient Rome*, *Ancient Greece*, *The Industrual Revolution*, *The Rise of the Nazis*, and *The Arab Spring Uprising*. The author's father, Israel Marcovitz, served in the US Army during World War II and in the closing months of the war was assigned to duty on the island of Okinawa. If atomic bombs had not been dropped on Japanese cities to end the war, Israel Marcovitz would have participated in the invasion of Japan.